ROAD TRIP

New Zealand

A guide for bikers, hikers, backpackers and drivers
using budget accommodation on both islands

Neil Foulks

First published in Great Britain in 2018
by
Neil Foulks
Copyright © Neil Foulks 2018

All photographs, unless otherwise stated,
are copyright Neil Foulks
Cover design by Neil Foulks

ISBN 978-1-912804-22-1

This paperback edition was printed by
Biddles Books, King's Lynn, PE32 1SF, UK
and is also available as an eBook.

To Mum

With thanks to:

Jake at RC8 Computers

John at Stormbringer Design

Nigel at Biddles Books

Vicki at Fool-proofs

Sam Manicom

and

Jacqui Furneaux, Ian Coates

and Elspeth Beard

for inspiring me to go in the first place.

Contents

Part One
NORTH ISLAND: Auckland to Wellington

Part Two
SOUTH ISLAND: Picton to Te Anau

A brief introduction

What started out as a motorcycle trip around New Zealand soon turned into a road trip by car and, without realising it, I had increased my audience to not only bikers, but also car drivers, backpackers and anyone who favours budget accommodation to keep costs down.

If, like me, you love to travel, then you will also have had to do some research on your destinations at some point, no matter how much you leave to the company you've booked through. Some of you are sticklers for perfection and would go screaming off to your holiday rep at the first sign of a construction site on the doorstep of your hotel, while others couldn't care less because they haven't booked ahead, and would have simply noticed that building site on arrival and moved on. Each to their own, I say.

Born of military parents in the early '70s, I quickly got used to moving house around Western Europe every few years, and changing schools became less of a problem as time moved on; the same could be said for making new friends. It really isn't an issue – you move on, you find your place in the social circle and you get on with things. So simple that a five-year-old could do it. I did.

From this, I never felt the need to 'belong' to anything and I realised that the less I belonged, the freer I was to do what *I* wanted to do. So that was marriage and kids out of the equation before I'd even reached puberty.

What I'm intending to do here is to lay down the bare bones of a trip to a beautiful country that most only ever visit once or twice - if at all - in a lifetime. There are, of course, other travel guides with more information on things I'm not too bothered about – like which bridge I would prefer to throw myself from for a huge fee – so I've made up my own, giving you as much information as I could gather while on my trip for you to work out your own itinerary and make it *your* trip.

Everywhere I stayed was for a maximum of two nights, so mostly I had just one shot at photographing every location – and if the weather was inclement, I had traffic up my backside or I couldn't stop for safety reasons, it was tough luck. My camera lived on the passenger seat at the ready.

You may still need to do more searching for what you want, as there's so much to do in New Zealand that I couldn't possibly begin to tell you what you should be doing – but all I can say is that everything I did in NZ, I enjoyed thoroughly. Every road I drove down, every switchback I took, every little village I stayed in – they have all made me want to come back again and do it by bike. Will I? HELL, YEAH!

I even left some things unfinished to ensure this will be the case.

So this is my account of my trip to New Zealand in early spring (September to October). I hope it will inspire you to do your own trip.

In the beginning...

It all started way back when I was 18, when I bought the Lonely Planet guide to New Zealand and read it cover to cover. Twice. I took it all in and a few places still stuck in my mind when I decided to do this trip nearly thirty years later. I gave the book to a friend back then, whom I didn't see again until fifteen years or so later. One Christmas I saw him in a pub in Dover and said,

'Where have you been all this time?' His reply was quite simply:

'Do you remember that book you gave me?'

My jaw dropped in anticipation, thinking that surely he wasn't going to say what he said next:

'I've got a wife and kids over there now. Cheers, Neil!'

I guess it just wasn't my time. So now, all these years later, here I am writing about my road trip and taking photos in the hope that I can give up the day job of being a deckhand in the merchant navy. It's not that I don't like the job – it's great but it's seasonal, and I believe I have other talents, which I can put to good use elsewhere. I'll do this until I find out what they are (laughs out loud).

I had originally planned to go to New Zealand and rent a motorcycle – any motorcycle. I'm not trendy or bothered about image, mileage or age, and I just planned to ride around NZ for a month or so, penning my journey and my experiences along the way, with a view to getting it in print somewhere after my return home. Taking photographs was also high on my priority list, as I could use them for an exhibition of my photography, which I have enjoyed doing as a hobby since my teens. I went to college back then, but I really only needed the second year of the two-year course, so I quit and went back to sea. Typical.

After a bit of research into bike/scooter rentals in North Island, and after reading the reviews, I knocked it down to the cheapest (what could go wrong?) and got a hire quote for a 250cc Yamaha Majesty scooter from the helpful guys at Scootling in Auckland for just under a month. With plenty of time and no need to rush, and room on the back seat for my grip, with my camping kit ready for the free campsites that are in abundance on the South Island, the resultant quote came in at $5–600.

I was hoping to tour both islands – until I read the small print and the 50km-a-day distance rule, at which point I had to look elsewhere, and the possibility of doing this trip on four wheels instead of two was very quickly becoming a reality.

Soon after, I was approached through social media by Colin Rowe of Pohutukawa Motorcycle Tours, via the Horizons Unlimited page on Facebook, and after we'd done the usual vetting of each other's profiles, I was offered the opportunity to write my story on my trip to New Zealand while promoting his tour company, which provides both guided and non-guided motorcycle tours of the USA and NZ. When I read the messages, I was completely gobsmacked that an opportunity like this should fall into *my* lap.

Colin turned out to be a Kiwi by birth, but now spends his time chasing the summer back and forth across the Pacific Ocean and giving his customers the ride of a lifetime, as either a fully guided or a more DIY, unguided affair, containing everything necessary to complete your trip, such as accommodation, tourist attraction entry, even some meals and so on. And with the hard work of deciding where to go taken out of the equation as well, what's not to like? Well, me being a budget traveller and not a fan of riding in groups of more than one, I had to turn to other means of making my way around the Land of the Long White Cloud. Motorcycle hire is expensive in most countries if you want a "proper" bike and New Zealand is no exception to this.

After the nightmare minefield of flight booking, I ended up in my local Thomas Cook shop and let them deal with it. It's funny, because when I worked in the North Sea and was constantly booking flights back and forth from Scotland to Spain, I never had a problem. But when you add in a stopover, the combinations multiply immeasurably, and the inevitable outcome is a fried brain and ending up right back where you started – so I left it to the pros. By all accounts, £800 is a pretty good deal for a return to NZ from the UK. Hide your biscuits, Cathay Pacific – here I come!

I sorted my spends through Asda Travel Money, as they're all pretty much the same price and you get two MasterCards, so the missus can rinse the account from hers and leave you devoid of beer tokens. Fortunately, I travel alone and I just needed a place to stash the spare card in case the unmentionable happened. I budgeted for about $120 a day, which wasn't enough, but there is always the backup. I planned to hire the car after seeing it first, as this is usually the way, isn't it? I never hired anything before seeing it first, except maybe a ladder.

The money was ready in a few days, to be picked up from a local Asda store – sign here, there and there. Job done – $2,100 to spend in-country. I hoped it would work.

Now all I needed to do was pack. Packing for a car is easy: open the trunk and chuck it all in. But for a bike? Well, this was still a possibility, albeit a small one, but I know how things usually turn out in my life and decided to take some bike kit anyway. Packing for a bike takes discipline and planning. The general rule of thumb here is that you go away with the kit you're actually going to use, rather than throwing things away mid-trip, or you will end up pulling stuff out of your bags when you return home, thinking 'I never used that' followed by a quick mental slapping with a reminder not to bring it next time.

I ended up with my waterproof roll-top sack with the camping gear in, my large rucksack with personal kit, footwear, cables and chargers, all with a combined weight of 23kg, and a carry-on bag full of tech, which definitely weighed more than the allowed 7kg. My Shad SB60 canvas bike panniers (the ones with the little trolley wheels and the pull-out handle you can lord it up with across the car park at the Premier Inn) – they were on the shortlist, but I didn't want them to become a burden in the event of me not being able to get my hands on a bike, so I left them behind to gather more mould in the shed.

After a hug and a kiss from Mum and a few grunts from Mitzi, the cat, I fired up the old 650cc Honda Deauville and set off towards Heathrow Airport over ninety miles away. The M25 is a necessary evil and my choice to ride to the airport was a snip of the price of the train, which came in at £69 whichever time I chose to travel. Parking at Heathrow was easily found round the back of Terminal 2, and it was under cover, so no need to put *another* exhaust burn into *another* rain cover. It's relatively secure and public, and the few bikers I met while I was there said they had seen bikes parked up for months on end with no trouble. Bargain. In hindsight, some of the other passengers' so-called hand luggage seemed to have the appearance of shipping containers. I could've got away with it after all. Maybe next time. At least my rain cover would be safe from being burnt again.

Days 1&2: The Flight

An overnight flight to Hong Kong was finished off with a local dish at O'Leary's bar in the airport – quesadillas with guacamole, sour cream and salsa, accompanied by a Leffe Braun Belgian beer. Not so nice the price, at £25, but it *was* tasty and I *would* need my Gaviscon tablets on the connecting flight to Auckland in a few hours. After another doze on another not-so-comfy couch, I chatted to Paul, a British expat who has lived in NZ for fourteen years. As well as working in the music industry as a critic, he also helps people who want to make the move 'down south', dealing with the usual mundane subjects of visas, removals and all the other stuff people would rather pay someone else to do for them. Some of us like the preparation and red tape – reminds me of that scene in *Father Ted*, when Mrs Doyle sums up her thoughts on tea-making with the line 'Maybe I *like* the misery'.

Finally, after another ten-hour flight, we touched down around lunchtime in Auckland and I was awake, on full alert, senses tingling in anticipation for what lay ahead. With my visitor's card filled in, I suddenly started wondering whether I needed a visa as, up until this point, it hadn't been mentioned. Because NZ is a Commonwealth country, I had just guessed I didn't need one. I needn't have been worried, as my thoughts were confirmed at immigration, where the machine automatically granted me a visitor's visa shortly before taking my mugshot and allowing me entry into New Zealand. The wait was over and the door to a new land was open. Was it Narnia? Or Middle Earth? Whatever. It was time to explore...

Part One

NORTH ISLAND: Auckland to Wellington

Days 3, 4 and 5: Auckland

Everything in New Zealand is expensive. Cigarettes' duty-free allowance is 50 – and they do sell packs of 50 cigs. It was a shame about the rolling tobacco coming in 30g pouches though. Fine – I found several e-cig shops online just in Auckland alone, so vaping it was, then. Until I got to about the second beer, then my resolve would break and I'd be back on the smokes. It's a disgusting habit, I know.

I met some great locals and not-so-locals in Father Ted's Irish Bar, who were all full of advice and tips. I learnt a bit about Kiwi politics and the recent (that day) elections – the things you don't 'see' when on holiday. I consider myself not a tourist, but a traveller. I don't follow the crowds and do all that jumping off of bridges and out of planes. I prefer to do it my way, bumbling along, getting lost and seeing where fate and karma lead me to, taking photos along the way in the hope that when people see them they'll say

'Where did you take that one?',

as opposed to the usual

'Oh, I've been there'.

It just doesn't make sense to me to go to a place you can see online, which has been photographed and documented a million times. In years to come, when you're reminiscing with your grand-kids, the images you recall could just as easily have been something you saw on TV yesterday.

Thanks to the bearded bloke behind the bar, Brian and Kirsten, plus Nooe from Mississippi, who added another angle when we were talking politics, it's always more interesting over a beer or three. I left after a good few beers, in the hope that my jet lag would pass quicker. It was only now that the need for solids had reared its head, just before bed. I don't remember eating the beginning of my burger, but I seemed to have woken up with my hands covered in melted cheese while still sat at the table under the Golden Arches. Cleaning myself up quickly to avoid embarrassment, I finished my burger (the remains of which were the two sloppy bits of bun left over after everything else had slipped out), rose and left, giving myself another mental slapping for not just going straight to bed in the first place. Incidentally, fast food in NZ is surprisingly cheap. Hopefully this won't turn into a cross between episodes of *Man vs Food* and *Supersize Me*.

My jet lag finally abated after a few days of being tired, eating at funny times and walking around the youth hostel like a zombie, just like most of the other guests at the hostel. It seemed like a quarantine for incoming tourists, who could only be released into the community when they were fully awake and at the correct time of day. There were many Europeans, mostly German, with Asian guests from Korea and China in good numbers. A lot of the Europeans were staying for a year after finishing high school, and were seeking work to make full use of their visas and to fund their trip.

No such luck for me, being over the working visa age of thirty. I would have to look at more permanent means. There was nothing stopping me looking for work while I was there – it's just that doing it would be slightly less than legal. It seems so unfair to cap it at thirty. If they allowed older people to come in on a working holiday visa, these people would generally have more skills, which would help the skills shortage – but I guess they want people to come and live there, not just pop over for a year. That said, they would have more expendable income to put into the tourist economy.

Sunday was the last day in the company of my young friends Hendrick (Mainz, Germany), Matz (France), Jun (China) and Bo Joon (Korea). Matz was a particularly interesting guy, who had spent the last two years cycling around Western Australia (he confessed to having a bit of a penchant for cycling across deserts), and had just taken delivery of his bike in Auckland, along with his girlfriend, who had just landed and he was starting a new job working at Mount Eden Park the day I left. It seemed he was all set for his next chapter, and jolly good luck to him.

The receptionist, Sasha, was extremely helpful with sourcing me a car, as I didn't have a credit card, which was required by most of the car hire companies (probably something to do with them being able to take any amount needed in case of any nasties happening).

Yes, it was decision time. I couldn't afford the cost of a 'proper' motorcycle, as I was looking upwards of $120 a day with the company Colin at Pohutukawa Tours had recommended.

There was no option of any discount, so I just had to go down the four-wheels route.

Actually, it was quite cool, because I had only passed my driving test less than a year ago, and wasn't able to hire a car in the UK until it had been a year, so I felt a bit of a rebel ('Rebel Without a Bike'). Besides, putting a time restriction on something like this seemed daft. While I know it's easier for the authorities to police, it seems stupid as far as the public are concerned, in so much as I might drive a thousand miles a week while you may only do that in a month. Who cares? I was getting me a wee car, and nobody was gonna stop me.

Day 6: Auckland to Kaiwaka – 168km

Usave Car and Truck Rentals was my saviour, and I popped down to their office first thing on the next morning as time was running out on my YHA stay. Not getting wheels sorted now could quite easily have resulted in an expensive hotel stay with my entire luggage, which was not an option. There was no need to fret, as Warren at Usave informed me that a simple $500 bond was all that was needed, which could be returned in exchange for a complete car at the end of my trip. The total cost of the Mazda Demio 1.2l came to $1,460 for 25 days of unlimited fun in the sun. I say 'sun' using the term loosely, as we were in the transition between winter and spring and the weather was quite unpredictable, although still reasonably warm by European standards.

Checking the car over for damage and taking the necessary photos, I bade Warren farewell and stuffed the road atlas he lent me into the glove box (I used the Kiwi maps *Pathfinder New Zealand Travellers Road Atlas*. Save your data on your cell phone and buy it for $34 on Amazon. This is an excellent guide), along with all the leaflets for the various visitor attractions on the North Island.

They really do all muck in in this country to help the tourism along. Everyone is so helpful in giving directions, opinions and generally being really nice and genuinely happy to meet you. It certainly does go a long way towards having a nice day.

By 10am I had returned to the youth hostel, double parked on the taxi rank outside, scraped a hub cap on the kerb, grabbed my kit, said my goodbyes and was off. With no idea in which direction I was headed, I just went uphill and followed the car in front, driving until I hopefully saw a sign for State Highway 1 heading north out of Auckland – and it wasn't long before I came across one. This city certainly was a joy to drive in. The rush hour there was no worse than my hometown of Dover in the UK.

Seeing a sign for Mount Eden, I remembered Matz telling me a bit about it and chucked a right up into the hills above the city, where the popular attraction takes the shape of an extinct volcano, of which there are dozens around Auckland, some inshore and some at sea. They make a great place to stretch your legs and get a panoramic view of the city. Above all, it's free, but you do have to walk to the top, which I was a bit hesitant to do, with my luggage in the car and not having a boot cover to conceal everything. While chatting to a Kiwi tour guide, I was given a quick spiel about the area and took a few photos and then I was off, leaving the guide to have to run to catch up with his clients. He pointed out One Tree Hill and I went all sentimental for a moment, knowing that Bono had probably been here.

Now I had my bearings, I headed towards the Auckland Harbour Bridge and north towards Whangarei. I had to tell myself that I couldn't just pop into every single place I saw along the way. It would take forever. I'd just go to the places that looked interesting to me, and not what the guide books said.

Travelling at 100km/h did feel quite slow, but the bonus of this was that I didn't get close to 3,000 rpm and burnt less fuel, plus I could enjoy the scenery more. I turned off the highway to avoid a toll, which was only about $2.40 for cars.

But even though the moths in my wallet would have barely woken up, I chose to avoid the toll and go for the path less trodden. I turned up a track as it looked interesting, and the notion that it would eventually lead to somewhere more interesting than a highway gave my spirits a lift.

It went on and on, with the odd turning into a property here and there, until the whole countryside opened up in front of me to reveal an almost Alpine lowland scene, with logging activity, little white farm houses with red roofs and short, lush, green grass. A chap on a dirt bike sped past me and nearly lost it on the corner – oh yes. This was a great place for biking, with its twists, hill climbs and sudden drops. Not high by any means, but definitely fun. This was the first place I got lost between leaving the road at Silverdale and heading up towards Wainui and across to Tahekeroa, where I asked directions from a passing lumberjack, who confirmed that I was indeed on the right route to the highway. Feeling chuffed with myself for not wasting too much time and getting lost even more, I stopped off at Puhoi to photograph the Catholic church, lost in a distant time, but well-maintained nonetheless. The nearby visitor attraction of Sheepworld was closed. Bummer. Some sheep-related japes would certainly have ensued. Instead, it was a water stop and the chance to check the map on my progress. What progress?

I had finally had enough just a few miles before Kaiwaka, after turning up a few tracks only to see the 'camping closed' sign one too many times. At the third attempt I saw a sign for Baldrock View Farm Stay and soon after I was greeted by Deanna, who was out levelling up some of her trees with her trusty sheepdog 'Pebbles'. She informed me that for the princely sum of $12.50, I could camp for the night. Shortly after I had eaten and showered, the sound of tyres crunching on gravel brought my attention to my new companions for the night. A French couple in an MPV with the ever-present sight of what looked like exploded suitcases in the back. After a greeting and a chat about which way both parties were headed, I slept early in a bid to wake later on and get some night-time photos of the valley. I didn't have any reference light source for the camera to meter on and tried in the almost pitch black, only using the light on my head torch to illuminate the fence line and my four-legged friend, who had no idea about standing still while I was taking a photo. Honestly, horses can be so dumb sometimes!

Woken by the horse at 2am, munching grass and whinnying to his pal across the field, I tossed and turned until I thought, 'Sod it. I'll pack and get off now if I can't sleep.' I tried to use the home made 10' x 10' cabin to make use of the only shower, only to find that the two Frenchies had used all the water. I'd have to fester for another day, I guess.

Day 7: Kaiwaka to Hotel Waipapakauri – 450km

An hour later I set off north on the State Highway 1 towards Whangarei, stopping for coffee in the only place open (McDonald's) and making my own when the opportunity allowed. I'm sure I missed some nice scenery on the way, but I was on a mission to get to the northernmost tip of New Zealand and head back down the west coast. So it was just me and the truckers for the first few hours, and let me tell you this – they don't take any prisoners, those truckers. If you're pulling out in front, you'd best be foot to the floor, because when they get within 100 feet of you (and they're pulling two trailer-loads of timber), that horn is proper loud! The Little Beast screamed in protest as I throttled every last ounce of power from her tiny engine, but I made it away and I'm still here.

Sunrise was a disappointment, greeting this part of the world at about 7am, due to the clocks going forward the previous week. Yes, it happens in NZ, too – and there was me thinking we only moved the clocks forward during the Second World War to help the farmers. Was this an April fool? I believed that spaghetti grew on trees until I was well into my twenties.

The main road in this country is little more than a two-lane affair (one either way, nothing fancy), which reminds me a lot of the A303 in Wiltshire with its overtaking sections and then going back to single lanes. It works because there isn't yet any reason to widen it, but I guess it's just a matter of time before they do as the population increases. Hopefully none of us will be here to see that day come.

The buildings became scarcer, the countryside more open and the forests bigger, until I came across a sign that said 'Gorge' on it, at which point I started to climb up... and up... and up. Twisty turns, switchbacks now and again, dodgy cambers, no crash barriers and narrowly missing the bull bars of the giant trucks coming down the other way. Fortunately, there was actually only one, but that was enough. One brown-trouser moment a day is enough for me, thank you. When the road levelled out at the apex, I had to stop for a breather to try to get my blood pressure back to normality and to take a few shaky photos.

The only thing worth photographing was a sign mentioning 'Kauri dieback'. It's a disease that affects these giant indigenous trees through people standing on roots and killing them, along with cross-contamination from other rainforests. The roots die off and then the tree follows suit. The sign simply told you to clean all of your gear before and after visiting the rainforest to help protect the Kauri. Poor Kauri.

Every single road here is motorbike heaven. I was told the reason that bike hire here is so expensive is due to the insurance, as there are so many accidents. Point taken.

The further north I went, the damper the climate became, and it wasn't too long before I saw signs for Ninety Mile Beach and the tip of the north – Cape Reinga. When you're on these one-way-in-and-one-way-out kinda roads, you keep seeing the same people and having these impromptu little catch-ups on your progress and the weather – the usual stuff, but handy if there's something you need to know about the road ahead. I couldn't actually see the road ahead because the mist had come down over the last three kilometres – and when I arrived at Cape Reinga, I couldn't see a bloody thing. I may as well have taken the photos at home in Morrisons car park. It was all I could do to take a few miserable-looking selfies on my mobile and make use of the public conveniences – which, I might add, in this country are very clean, with only a hint of graffiti. No needles, beer cans, roaches or malicious damage here. Obviously the kids have better things to do. And good luck to 'em.

So that was it. The proper start point had been reached and now all I had to do was head south. That seemed easy enough, but what I really needed to do now was some laundry, and that evening I wanted to take some photos of Auckland Harbour and the city skyline at night. You cannot avoid the city if you are travelling south. There are still plenty of other places where a bridge could be put in – like from Little Hula to Wattle Bay for instance, but what do I know? All I know is that I have a date with a bridge and my dirty pants. Life is so hard sometimes, it kills me.

I popped into Ahipara at the southern tip of Ninety Mile Beach just to fulfil a teenage dream of standing there. Yup, it's a beach. I looked out to sea and mentally ticked the box that said that sea was indeed the Tasman Sea. Well done me for finally making it. And no, this wasn't a 'bucket list' thing – I don't have a bucket list because I have no intention of dying yet.

I backtracked to a hotel I had passed a while ago at Waipapakauri, for no other reason other than its name sounded like 'wipe up a curry', and enquired about a room. I met a nice Maori woman, who was smoking on the front steps of the one-storey working men's club/village pub/pool room/farmers' hangout – you get the gist – who told me that the rooms were cheap and that her and her husband were happy with theirs, so I deemed that fine and checked in. At $36 it was a bit more than the youth hostel, but hey, I was getting a full-on Kiwi-style digs experience and not mixing with fellow Europeans for a change. The clientele were mostly from the farming community, some in just their socks, having left their muddy boots on the porch. By the state and smell of them, they should've left their coveralls there too. Bad image?

There was a pool competition going on in the adjoining room and tempers were getting a bit frayed, with shouts and whooping and hollering as balls were potted. I was too tired to have much more interest than that. I would've fancied a game of pool, as it had been so long, but when there's another team in, you'll never get a look-in until they've finished. One massive burger and a bucket of fries later (they put beetroot – yes, BEETROOT – in the burgers here, and by all accounts it fits quite well), plus a few pints (they call them 'handles' – more on this later) of local brew, and I was ready for bed. I tried to discipline myself into doing some writing, but I think I'm better attuned to doing this as soon as I get up, as this is when I'm at my most creative. Make of that what you will.

Day 8: Waipapakauri to Auckland YHA – 323km

After a decent night's kip with fleece blankets instead of sheets (it must get proper cold up here in winter), I awoke and readied myself for the drive back to Auckland. On packing the car and having a cup of cornflakes from my HM Prison Service plastic mug, I noticed a propeller mounted on a plinth at the end of the car park, marking a war memorial to the New Zealand RAF, who were stationed here during WWII, along with many ground troops to boost the defences against any invasion from the Japanese after the bombing of Pearl Harbour in 1941. I felt duty-bound to pay my respects for a few moments and to take the obligatory photos, before leaving Waipapakauri for Auckland. Back down SH1, past all the places I had already seen. Head down, arse up on my return to the city of the Orcs.

Having downloaded the 'Offline Maps' mobile app map of New Zealand onto my tablet, I decided to give it a run – and as there aren't that many roads here, it seemed to work quite well. Operator error is a large factor in any mechanical/ electrical issue, and that morning it seemed to not want to play ball – the darned thing wanted me to download the map again. Back to the old-school and the road atlas. Even I couldn't get lost in... oh, wait – I already did. 'Temporarily misplaced' is my preferred term, I think.

I wanted to avoid the Mangamuka Gorge this time and skirt around its southern side, heading down towards Rawene for the car ferry and then joining the SH12 back to the SH1, but the sat nav had different ideas – and I really needed to make tracks if I was going to get back to Auckland before dark.

The question of my laundry was becoming ever more of an issue, and I plumped for the little suburb of Kamo, just outside Whangarei. A fully automated affair greeted me, along with a change machine that took notes. So I put in the smallest note I had, which just happened to be a $50. I received $50 worth of laundry tokens for the machines. ARSES! These things are put here to test us, I suppose. I did get my laundry done and I managed to palm a few of the unwanted tokens off to other users. With clean clobber and a marginally tidier boot, I had a spot of lunch and a quick nap and then it was time to do the off again.

By avoiding the toll road (there are only three in the whole country), you can take the scenic route as opposed to the 'proper' route through the tunnel, which is what you'd be paying the toll for. The free route takes you over the top of the hills to Waiwera and down to Hatfields Beach, passing over the Puhoi river estuary – I cocked this part up and ended up following the side roads to finish up at Northcote Point, fuming at my navigational error. There is always a diamond in the shit, and my diamond was right in front of me, as I was greeted with an awesome view of the Auckland Harbour Bridge, with the sun setting behind the city beyond. I loved the place names around this place. 'Birkenhead' was nothing at all like its namesake – more of an improvement on the original, and they do actually keep a few grey ships in Devonport. New Zealand's whole naval fleet is probably there.

On pulling off at junction 423, heading south across the Harbour Bridge, I saw a guy with a tripod taking pictures of the city skyline and parked up at my first opportunity. I grabbed my camera bag and doubled back on myself, past some really stunning properties – with views like this, they must be worth millions. I kept telling myself that this was stuff I could do when I'd handed the car back in the last few days of my trip, but screw it – I was here now, so I may as well have made the effort, because it could be raining next time.

Next stop was already on the cards, I guess. Back to the youth hostel for a charge-up, proper cooking and a good night's kip. Well – I got one of them right. 'Proper cooking' turned out to be a posh pot noodle with a kiwi fruit, yogurt and a beer – my last Heineken, as the kitchen was mega busy and I had writing to do and photos to edit. I didn't have the best night's kip, but I did have a dorm to myself, so all was not lost. If only they had tables in the rooms, I could've written in my pants, all relaxed. Hendrick and Matz were surprised to see me back so soon, but I had done with the north and it was time to move on. Sleep got the better of me, and I soon had to finish up and head for my pit.

Day 9: Auckland to Whangamata Surf n Stay – 318km

At 6:30am, it was time to do the off. After a quick breakfast of something quite similar to the night before, I checked out and headed off into the 'rush hour', travelling ever southwards and then east across to the highly recommended Coromandel Peninsula, which was recommended by Colin at Pohutukawa Tours, along with many friends, and is commonly billed as having probably the best riding roads in all of New Zealand. It's no wonder that the Kiwis have a bad reputation for their driving. Two words come to mind: 'lane' and 'discipline'. You'll see what I mean.

Eventually, the main road became single-file, and I sat back with the tunes full on, singing along to Green Day and winding my way through the lanes towards the town of Thames and the road to the Coromandel Peninsula. The tops of the hills were covered in a thick mist, making photography a bit of a challenge. More black and white photos, then.

The road soon turned into a roller-coaster, but a roller-coaster that had two-way traffic, and you could bet your bottom dollar that whatever was coming around that blind bend – and there were hundreds – was going to be at least double your size – and that's exactly what happened. All of a sudden, I was on the brakes and staring like a rabbit into the headlamps of an oncoming logging truck. With a trailer. Up and down and around and around. If twisting roads and hairpins are your thing, then New Zealand will *not* disappoint, I can tell you that much. I spent the next few hours with one eye glued to the white line on my left so as not to go overboard and have an early bath, and the other eye watching for anything coming around the corner. Concentrating so hard made me forget to breathe and gave me a headache. I wished I was on a bike, with all that extra wiggle room to play with, but it wasn't meant to be and I had to opt for the staying-dry and queuing-up route. At least parking for cars is pretty much free in NZ. There is pay and display parking, but nowhere near what we're used to in Europe. Bike parking is free everywhere, as usual, as you cannot put a paid parking ticket on a bike. I think it's got something to do with the lack of doors and a roof to stop the ticket just blowing away, but I may be wrong.

I digress. There are plenty of lay-bys where you can take a few photos or just get the hell out of the way of the 30-ton truck behind you. Everything seems to be so well thought-out here. I couldn't pinpoint things off the top of my head, but you'll notice little things on your way around and go, 'Ah. That's neat. Why don't they do that where I live?'

Eventually, Coromandel came into view and I turned uphill and inland to cross the peninsula and headed down to Whitianga, where I turned right, picking up the SH25 and heading south on more bendy roads. There is a youth hostel at Opoutere, and by the time I had found it I was quite jiggered and just needed to get some proper rest, as I had been writing, taking photos and driving more than I had ever done. There was only one problem. No youth hostel. Well, it was there, but locked up, with half the boundary fence ripped down as though someone had come around the corner too fast and driven straight into it. It appeared that the youth hostel at Opoutere was only open part-time.

I just had to muster up some spirit to get me to somewhere I could put up my tent and get some proper rest. As luck would have it, I came across a B&B only a few kilometres up the road towards Whangamata.

Then, keeping the yin in equal balance with the yang, the bad luck was that when I spoke to the most beautiful Kiwi lady of the trip so far, she informed me that her dad, who runs the B&B, had just had heart surgery and wasn't taking bookings at the moment. Seemed fair enough, but I wanted a bed! She told me to go to Whangamata, as it was closest and much better than Waihi. So the seed was sown. Whangamata it was. And oh, what a good choice.

The Surf n Stay surfers' and backpackers' hostel was a minute's walk from the beach, where I took some of the most stunning photos yet. The sun rises here from way over in the Pacific Ocean, and the two islands make a great photo opportunity. There are no locks on the doors at the backpackers' lodge – no crime here, boyo. I was a bit concerned, but my fears were dispelled when I saw the house prices in the area. Ah, there was my answer – $500,000 plus for anything remotely posh. Lots of holiday homes for the Auckland folk.

After originally driving around town a bit, and being offered a bed for $135 at the dearest accommodation in the town, the chap informed me about the backpackers and the other B&Bs, which floated my boat very nicely indeed. I didn't bother with the web and insisted on going into places to get a feel of them and have a chat with some locals. They had plenty of time on their hands at that time of year, so why not? It was amazing, the amount of expats there. I met people from Kent, people from Northumberland, Cornwall and Northern Ireland. I had a walk around all the usual shops you'll see frequently in a Kiwi seaside town. The only difference was in the names, but one shop stood out.

A picture-framing and printing store by the cinema was where I had to go and check out the local photographic talent. I had already taken some stunning photos of the sunrise on Whangamata beach, with the two islands in the shot. There were other versions, but I preferred my own. I spoke to the owner, an elderly chap who claimed most of the images as his. We spoke about cameras and nice places to photograph. It seemed I had already taken the best shot of the local area.

The only other place to take good photos was apparently from inside Doughnut Island, the smaller of the two in my photo, and about one kilometre from the beach – an easy paddle by SUP or kayak. I could borrow a dry bag from Surf n Stay and hire a sit-on kayak for $35. I decided I would leave this for when I returned, as money was tight and I couldn't think of a better excuse.

Day 10: Whangamata – 0km

Friday was turning out to be a great day of relaxing (and not hurrying into the car at stupid o'clock in the morning to get some miles under my belt before breakfast), but breakfast had finished a few hours ago and now it was approaching noon, which could only mean one thing – BEER O'CLOCK! After a bit of searching, I found Bucks Sports Bar and Grill – essentially a betting shop with beer and food. What more could any discerning Kiwi need to escape the missus and watch the footie and the racing?

Maxine was an excellent host along with locals Sue and Dave, who filled me in on local events, and we chatted about things back in the UK – everyone seemed interested to know what us Brits think about Brexit. My reply is always short and sweet: 'At the end of the day, we still have to get up in the morning and pay tax.'

One mutant chicken burger and far too many fries later, Maxine came over and asked if it was OK.

'What did you think of the beetroot I put in it?' she asked. 'I know it isn't normal for you British folks, but I put it in anyway to see how you'd react.'

'I like it!'

Maybe it'll catch on in the UK – well, I guess I should bring *something* home. The main problem for me here was the beer. As an ale drinker, there are a few micro-breweries, but they're not called that and it still has fizz in it. So it was craft lager or craft ale then, I supposed. There is some good stuff in bottles in the supermarkets, though – I found four bottles of Fursty

Ferret Ale from the Badger Brewery at $2.99 each and bought the lot. All the way from England and at that price, too. How was this even possible?

A 900ml bottle of Kiwi ale will normally set you back about $12, which isn't too shabby. The prices of fresh fruit and veg are extortionate in NZ. I guess the only way to bring them down would be to breed more people. Given the state of some other countries, I would be happier to live with the alternative and pay out more. Three beers later (or 'handles', which come in various different sizes – what you see is what you get) and I was ready for a siesta.

That evening, more surfers came down from Auckland for the weekend, and much chatting was had about extreme sports, mountain biking and such like, bringing back memories of my twenties. All I could bring to the table was stories of old stars of the sport, which were met with blank looks and then carrying on their conversation. The beer flowed and we all got along nicely, though. Numbers were exchanged and a free surfing session was offered to me. The Belgian guy even had a large wetsuit he was happy to lend me, as it was his brother's, who wasn't coming.

Day 11: Whangamata to Bledisloe – 212km

I checked the surf in the morning after my 6am rise to photograph the sunrise again, and it was as they said – bigger than yesterday. It looked a bit blown-out to me, so as I was up and dressed I decided to go one step further and pack the car ready for the off after a hearty breakfast.

Sure enough, the spotty German Woofer (stands for working for food and accommodation, etc.) came down and started cleaning up the lounge areas while I was getting under her feet and asking for bread for the toaster. I should've been less selfish and stayed out of her way, but the way I saw it was that I was one less person to cook eggs for. I'd be back for Doughnut Island another time, but right then I had tracks to make.

I had intended to head for Napier, Hastings and Gisborne, but during the night I had the great idea of doing an online search for the ferry prices from Wellington to Picton across the Cook Straits, and was shocked when a figure of over $200 came up. EACH WAY! I didn't think it was going to be anywhere near this, as while researching the car hire prices, I saw that a lot of them offer it as an add-on just in case you intend to head south. You can also hire snow chains for your car for a reasonable price, but the ferry add-on was a mere $72 or something when selected at the time of making the car booking. That offer had gone now, but I ended up getting my ticket a few days later in Ohakune for less than I could find it online. That was the second time someone in the high street (the local i-Site, New Zealands' tourist information service) had booked my ticket and saved me money.

However, I didn't have a great day behind the wheel and only made it as far as Little Waihi Beach, just south of Tauranga, to a place called Bledisloe Camping at Maketu, which I eventually found after a few wrong turns and a bit of swearing, located right down on the beach, with water on three sides. It was $16 a night to pitch my tent, with the use of two large shower blocks (showers are token-operated) and, as I found later when I walked around the other side of my shower block, quite a large kitchen, with four pub picnic tables in the middle. There were also work surfaces around the outside walls for preparing and cooking food, and a few sinks on the opposite side. Sorted. I charged all of my toys, wrote a few more pages on my progress while supping a bottle of beer, and then it was lights-out time.

At about 4:30am, I woke up, wondering if it was still clear in the heavens – and, to my amazement, I was greeted with an almost perfect view of the galaxy, much brighter than I had seen before, probably due to the lack of light pollution. It was a shame about the light from the ablutions block behind me, but it didn't stop me taking my first ever photo of the stars with a camper van. Pleasantly chuffed, I went back to bed for a bit and then thought,

'Sod it, I'm up now. I may as well saddle up and do the off.'

Day 12: Bledisloe to Ohakune – 270km

Quietly sneaking out of the campsite at 5:30am, with the voice of the owner nagging away inside my head saying 'Nobody leaves before 7am', I was hoping that the key for the lock fitted both turnstiles to let me out. It did, and I was away. Full beams on, tunnel vision, twisting, turning, undulating roads back up the hill towards Te Puke, State Highway 33 and down to Rotorua. I went around the ring road, not bothered about stopping off anywhere to play the tourist – not on a Sunday morning, at any rate. Most places don't open until ten. What I did see were several plumes of steam coming up from the sides of the road, and I knew what they were: sulphur pools – part of Planet Earth's cooling system, where Mother Nature quite literally 'lets off steam'. I parked up in a lay-by and nipped out, camera in hand, and skirted the barrier fencing for the builders, where they were doing more road repairs. Hats off to those boys and girls for keeping the roads open. It's just a shame that the earthquake of 2016 has still left some damage, hence the closure of SH1, which won't be finished any time soon – so check before you come on over by visiting the NZ government traffic and travel website.

I took a few photos and then it was back to the car, towards Taupo on SH5. As I followed the shoreline of North Island's biggest lake, it started raining, and very soon I was pre-composing photographs in my head.

It was only at the end of the lake, when I came across an old man fishing in a fast-flowing river estuary in a pair of waders, water up to his chest, when I noticed a photo opportunity and rose to the challenge. I had already decided to make this a black and white photo, so camera settings and new maths were being churned around in my head at the same time as turning the car around in the road.

After a quick brew, it was time for more bendy, windy roads down Waiouru way and back onto SH1 again. I saw from my road atlas that the Army Museum was also there, so I made a mental note to pop in at some point.

The main reason for going this way was because there is a youth hostel at Ohakune and I had had enough for one day. Only another 27km from the main highway to get a nice warm bed, shower and a meal cooked in the kitchen at the Station Lodge Hostel. I tried to find the Army Museum, but my tiredness was getting the better of me, so I just headed straight for the hostel instead.

Through the mist and the rain I saw the Lodge, which I felt was very Wild West. Not really that dissimilar to the old stand-alone Victorian stations I remember in Kent from when I was a kid – derelict ones, which sometimes ended up being sold privately to people who wanted to live somewhere a bit quirky. The railway company make some money from a sale of property and the eyesore gets a facelift, which the council don't have to put their hands in their pockets for (as Rik Mayall used to say, 'Thatcher's Bloody Britain'). This one, as it's not in Britain, has been kept open and running and is in pretty good shape, keeping that old colonial vibe going for a few more decades yet, I hope.

After a siesta, I went out for some supplies in the town and realised I was in the middle of the North Island's version of Aviemore in Scotland. IT WAS A SKI RESORT! AWESOME!

New Zealand never failed to surprise me. I had only looked on the map for a cheap place to lay my head, and as my map didn't show contours I had no idea, but you could've guessed, like – tallest peak on the island and all that.

With names including 'Lodge' and 'Peaks' and 'Alpine', I saw shops selling boards, skis and all the other kit that winter sports enthusiasts like to spend their hard-earned cash on, but no amount of money could change the weather, and most people just came to try their luck, as it was still school holidays (the kids get their long six-to-seven-week holidays in their summer - over Christmas - and have a few weeks off in between terms, with no half-term holidays like in the UK).

I found a New World supermarket, which had been described to me as 'as near as NZ gets to Marks and Spencer'. I think he was just referring to their prices. Just like everywhere else in NZ, it was expensive, but they had most things you'd want on a road trip. Bottled beer isn't too costly in comparison, and if wine is your tipple then be prepared to have a field day. The average price for a bottle of plonk is $10 or thereabouts. It's only when you go into the pubs in the larger cities that it hits you hardest. The Kiwi 'handle' of beer isn't a unit of measurement like the British pint is, with its 568ml standardised size – the handle is more a 'what you see is what you get', as they can range from 450ml to just under a pint, and different 'heads' come into it as well. I've paid $7 for a handle in Whangamata at Bucks, but just be aware of this, as you will get confused when you get different answers if you ask the question in different drinking parlours.

Back at the Station Lodge, we cooked, we ate and we chatted. All from different nations, speaking about places we had been or planned to visit, each adding their input to the constant flow of information flying around the room amidst the aromas of the evening meals from kitchens across the globe.

That night, while chilling on the free wifi, I had a proper look at the ferry prices. It resulted in $208 each way which was a budget-blowing price to pay, but I knew it had to be done – otherwise this was going to be a short trip, indeed. The only thing for it would be to haul ass to Wellington in the morning and get a ferry the following day. I could fill in some time by going to see a contact I had made at the Maritime Union of New Zealand (MUNZ) about work possibilities on a permanent basis as well. Double-whammy.

I got chatting to an English bloke called Ollie, who was in his twenties and came across as a bit camp, but who was I to judge? He was going to Wellington as well, but at my offer of a lift not long after we met, he turned it down and – well, you know how it is. Awkward. So, not being used to that kind of situation, I left it at that.

The subject of Mount Tongariro came up, along with who was going up to make use of the facilities. I said that I was keen to go up if anyone wanted a lift and, surprise, surprise, Ollie piped up and we agreed to drive as far as the road would let us and see if we could get any decent photos of, well, anything that wasn't covered in cloud. We agreed a time and a place to meet in the morning, and shortly afterwards everyone went to bed. Even the Brazilians, Freddy and Jessica, came back from the pub in time to say goodnight. 'Goodnight.'

Day 13: Ohakune to Wellington – 290km

I met Ollie after I'd packed up, and we breakfasted together after accidentally taking the Chinese guests' table when they had their backs turned while preparing breakfast noodles. I had a more traditional British fare of cereal, yogurt and fruit – nothing too exciting, but it did the job.

Ollie was on his way to Wellington to pick up his car, and was doing it by the open-top tourist train at great expense, but it was what he wanted, so fair play – to each his own and all that. He'd be telling me he rides a Harley next. I did ask if he was a train 'enthusiast', to which he replied mostly in the positive. 'This is gonna be fun,' I thought – two blokes going up a mountain and all that. A penny dropped, far off in the distance. Two blokes up a mountain? Didn't they make a film about that?

Leaving a bit early, we hit the road into the town for only 100m, then it was a right turn at the pub and over the bridge and straight uphill. Piece of cake. Even I couldn't get this wrong. The little car protested at taking a passenger by offering me almost no power on the steeper inclines, with the added extra weight – first gear was used a few times. I wished I had my Shogun here now. She'd love this, old Mitzi the Mitsubishi. But the Little Beast was great on fuel, so I couldn't knock her. I'd lose my bond if I did.

We pulled over a few times as we entered the snowline and took pictures of each other posing with the signs, thinking we weren't going to get much further – until some other vehicles drove past us and carried on up. We followed, only to realise that we had stopped on the last corner before the plateau, with a car park with about 100 cars in it. Parking attendants were stopping people going right to the top, as the clouds were dropping visibility right down. 'So why the hell are people skiing, then, if they can't see sod all?' I asked Ollie. I did ask a few parents when we went into the site, with its huge cafe littered with miscellaneous hats, gloves, bags and boots and with the windows all misted up with condensation. They all replied with similar reasoning: Lift passes needed to be used up, as it was the last week of the season. Fair enough. I guess it's kitted out for year-round use, by the looks of the snow machines at the top of the slopes, but you can't beat the real thing.

More photos were taken and Olly was keen to get pics of the kids on their slope. It has a conveyor belt running up the side of it, instead of a ski lift. I guess it's for safety reasons. You just stand on the belt and up you go.

With the low cloud came a light rain, carried on a cold wind and making the use of photography equipment a bit of a challenge. Nothing that a 'Nelson's arm in his jacket' couldn't solve. It proved a bit difficult with my 200mm lens on, though.

We left after an hour or so of messing about on things we shouldn't have in the name of candid photography, and had a mandatory coffee to warm our hands and buy bike stickers. We then returned to the Wee Beast and descended the mountain much quicker than when we went up.

Back into the town of Ohakune, we visited the Chocolate Eclair Shop, which Ollie really had to twist my arm to get me to go to. Not. The biggest chocolate eclairs I have ever had and they were selling like hot cakes. He wanted one for the train conductor and I wanted one for Ron (later Ron). We then went on a giant carrot hunt in the park behind the shop (Ohakune's other claim to fame is being the carrot centre of New Zealand), and it wasn't long before a giant carrot greeted us – all 30-odd feet of it. Taking a selfie and fitting that all in wasn't easy, but we succeeded. There was also a potato, an onion and a sprout in the kids' play area. Well, it's one way of getting your children to eat their veggies, and if it works, then that's great.

We popped into the i-Site, New Zealand's tourist information office, and enquired about my ferry ticket. I managed to get the girl to come up with a quote for $80 less than my online search. Sweet. I booked it there and then, safe in the knowledge that the prices would rise the closer it got to sailing day. Happy with my purchase, I dropped Ollie off back at the hostel and said goodbye to the sweet little German Woofy, who was most upset when I told her we'd been up the hill to see the skiing. A very petite size six or eight at the most, she was also a keen snowboarder, and worked at the hostel looking after it most of the time as the owners were away a lot – it was up for sale soon, too. It would be like owning a pub or having kids, though. Seven days a week, 365 days a year. Not for me, thanks.

Heading back to the SH49, which would take me the 27km back to SH1 at Waiouru where the Army Museum was, I topped up with gas and pulled in and had lunch in the museum café, after paying my very modest $15 entry fee. The life-size mannequins and arsenal of weaponry on display was quite impressive, along with the battle honours of many who had fought and died for New Zealand and the Commonwealth.

There was plenty to photograph, read and digest – well worth a visit and, as it's value for money, it's a must.

Time was getting on; I had an open road with little traffic and good visibility, and still had a few hundred clicks to do, so it was time to put my foot down. But someone else had other ideas and, as he came over the horizon his blues and two's were already flashing. How do they do that? I looked at the clock and it was a fair cop. When I looked in the rear view mirror, in the vain hope that his concern lay somewhere else and I was about to get away with it, he dispelled that idea and spun around in the road, gunning it to catch me up. Well, this was a first.

I pulled over and wound down my window. From greeting to leaving the scene of the crime with my payment card took about three minutes. Job done.

'Will I get points on my licence?' I asked.

'No, because you're foreign,' he replied.

My instant reply was to turn to him with both thumbs up and go -

'Yeah!', quickly followed by a 'Thank you, Sir. Sorry, Sir. I'll keep my speed down in future.'

Nice chap. Remember the $80 I saved on my ferry ticket? Same price as a speeding ticket. I may not have been having a great day in the wallet, but it was OK, because karma was having a right good laugh at my expense.

Eventually, after passing several townships on the State Highway 1, Palmerston North being the only one I could pronounce, I came to Wellington and found the youth hostel quite easily. They had space. Yay! I never book ahead, leaving it to fate to decide where I end up. I only decide where to go the next day, over breakfast or when I get in the car. This usually increases the chance of an adventure of some description. Added to this, I don't use the sat nav unless in city centres, and spend a lot of my time getting lost – as you already know only too well.

After a shower, I carried out the ritual of labelling my food in bags with the supplied YHA food labels, and made sure not to use the 'free food' shelf to store my dry goods. The kitchen was full of extremely animated young Italians cooking pasta. It was quite a sight. The girls were making up the tables and the boys were all stood around the stove – about ten of them – shouting instructions at the elected 'cook' with the spoon. I left them to it and used the microwave to sort my dinner out. You'd never see this with British kids. They just got on and did it – it was a pleasure to watch. Credit to their parents. I just had noodles, coffee and kiwi fruit.

I shared my room that night with a very well-spoken chap of 32 from the UK and a German/Scot (nice mix). Both were quite well educated and could've passed for army officers, no problem.

Day 14: Wellington to Picton (South Island) – 3km

Every night when speaking with the people I met, they almost all said that the South Island is where it's at. And today was the day. First, though, I needed to go where my roomies mentioned last night: Mount Victoria – just behind the YHA and up the hill, where I could get some awesome photos of the sun rising and a bird's-eye view of the city. I raced up the hill (in the car – I'm not mad. Although I wouldn't have been alone, as there were a few dozen joggers doing their morning exercise), and made the top in time to get a few shots of the city in the early hours before light. I moved on up into the viewing platform right at the top of Mount Victoria and waited for the sun.

A young Asian couple were standing in front of me, arm in arm, while I could only cradle my camera. Another memory of the best part of the day, and a few more shots, while witnessing all the ladies taking their selfies with their smartphones and the sunrise burning out their backgrounds. I couldn't wait to edit these photos, but it was time to hit the road, I guessed.

After a quick room sweep through cupboards and drawers and under my bed and duvet to make sure I left with everything I came with, I left the other two to their dreams, went down the six floors to reception and ordered one of their breakfasts, which consisted of a coffee and a bagel with cream cheese and jam. Yummy. All for $6 less per night than the Auckland hostel, but on mentioning this I was informed by a Lancashire lad at reception that things were being standardised. I had to get my groove on or I would end up with a parking ticket, so I had a quick munch, checked the map and off I went.

I decided to visit the Maritime Union for New Zealand (MUNZ for short) office in the town centre and find out what the score was down here with regard to British seafarers finding work. The bottom line was that there wasn't much about. I planned to keep my nose to the ground and my ears open. I had a few more contacts now, which is always good.

I headed for the ferry terminal, which is in the centre of town and a much more pleasant affair than Dover–Calais, in so much as that you are not in a cornered market. You can park out the front of the booking office with Bluebridge and you can just nip into town to do whatever. Just be back an hour before the sailing time. I was back well ahead of that, and subsequently first in the queue – but not for long, though, as the girl in the hi-vis directing traffic onto the quayside told me to go to the end of the quay and get in lane one. I went to the end of the quay and... I couldn't see the markings on the bloody tarmac. Where's lane one? Rather than sit there like an idiot, I drove back the 50 metres to the girl and asked her again what she meant – just as the second car came along, so I followed that instead. It turned out she just wanted me to come back to the top, about five metres from where she was standing. Duh!

We sat there for well over an hour and then the deck officer started loading the cars after the trucks had been loaded from their parking area. It was a hot afternoon. The lack of any ozone layer in NZ really makes the sun burn on any exposed flesh, and I was beginning to wish I'd bought some sun tan lotion. Instead, I'd have to put up with 'taxi driver's elbow' from resting my forearm on the window sill. 'Slip, slap, slop' is a must in the summer months, though, if you don't want to end up like Joan of Arc.

Finally, we loaded, and it was another first for me as I'd only ridden two-wheelers onto the deck of a ferry before. This was turning out to be a bit of a busman's holiday.

The view on leaving the harbour at Wellington was very pleasant, and I managed a series of photos in order to make one of my high resolution panoramic images from the stern looking towards the city skyline, shortly before it went out of view and we headed into the Cook Strait.

The food on the Bluebridge Straitsman was OK. The choice was very similar to what I had been serving up for customers on the cross-channel ferries from the UK to France only a few months previously – fish and chips, curry, a veggie option, the usual stuff. Prices were similar, but the curry wasn't a patch on the P&O chicken tikka masala – that's so good, even the crew eat it. I couldn't finish it all and that's saying something, coming from a fat lad.

A walk on the outer decks and I got chatting with a truckie, who was also a biker. That was me sorted for the trip, then. I managed to glean a lot of information from him as we spoke about the roads, the cost of bikes in NZ, places to visit and so on. The sun was shining and I could see snow on the tops of the mountains that welcomed us into Picton. This place reminded me of the Fjords in Norway. This was probably why I hadn't seen any Norwegians here yet. A tiny town, but with plenty of character, nonetheless. It was a stark contrast to

Wellington, which is a bit strange – as the majority of visitors go to both islands, you would've thought it would be similar in size, but no, that just isn't the case. Cattle, wood, tourists and not much else here, apart from a few places to get your head down.

I tried to find the place that Freddy, the Brazilian at the Station Lodge YHA, had told me about, but with no luck. Instead, I stumbled across The Villa, an affiliated youth hostel with more character than anywhere else I had stayed so far. This place oozed the chill factor. Painted in a light blue, with added outbuildings for extra bed space, I was serenaded onto the porch by a beautiful girl playing a guitar. Shame her playing wasn't as good as her looks – but then I can't talk, the way I play bass.

For little more than the equivalent of ten of my English pounds, I had a bed in a mixed ten-person dorm. Who wants to camp when it's this cheap? Free wifi and a full kitchen, spa and even a tree house in the garden. I later found out that the guitar being played belonged there, too. Sweet. But it seemed that the travelling community of New Zealand was safe in the knowledge that I couldn't deafen them with my noise, as the chances of anyone having a lefty bass knocking about were quite slim.

After we had all eaten at 8pm, the sound of bell-ringing, followed by an announcement of 'Come and get your free apple crumble and ice cream', echoed around the house, as people peeled their eyes away from their various electronic devices and dragged themselves from their perches and made their way to queue for a pretty damned good homemade pudding, with a choice of vanilla or boysenberry ice cream. I was asked by one girl 'What's boysenberry? I've never had it'.

To which I naturally rose to the opportunity to be a proper sarcastic tit and replied,

'It's like girlsenberry, but with boys in it.'

This was followed by the thud of a lead balloon.

Most retired to the lounge, where the talk was of the usual travel nature, and when all were done with their bowls, most people washed them up then slid off back to their little boxes with pictures in.

Bedtime loomed and people disappeared slowly, one by one. I had laundry to sort out and had no opportunity to use my bagful of tokens, so had to use cash. Damn. Washing took ages, in which time I got chatting with a girl from Manchester who was next in line after me, about her job as a social worker for the NZ equivalent of the NHS. You meet all sorts in these places. I got up to go and check on the drying and bumped into this little wiry bloke with a goatee beard, who greeted me with

'G'day, mate!'

I said 'hi' to him and we started talking about trucks – his in particular. He was carrying 300 bulls from Christchurch to Auckland and had missed his ferry.

'Did your boss give you a bullocking?' I asked, jokingly.

'A little bit, yeah,' was his reply. 'You see, if I give 'em a feed, they'll stay stood up, but if they go down, they find it hard to get up, then they die by being trampled on by the other bulls. Not a nice way to go.'

He was telling us his anecdotes of the day as he had to load the bulls himself, due to his colleague being off sick. Chasing the last bull around the paddock is apparently not fun. I bet it is if you're not in there with it!

We had a giggle about the whole episode and went to bed. I woke up for a midnight toilet trip and bumped into him again at the door, trying to open it with his key, not realising there weren't any locks on the doors. I'm sure he was a bit drunk. He must've had a few scoops on the way back from the docks.

'I just checked 'em, and of the four that had fallen over, three are now dead.'

Harsh. At $500 a bull, that wasn't good news for his boss.

Auckland Harbour Bridge

Boat jetty at Akaroa

It's amazing what you see in people's front gardens

The Trip Inn, Westport

On the way to Milford Sound

Massive sand dunes at Ninety Mile Beach

Chequered Flag Bar near Christchurch

Franz Josef Glacier doing its disappearing act

I love these campers' personal touches

Gunn Lake, Milford Sound

Irishman Creek, Canterbury Plains

Tourists soak up the view on the way down into Queenstown

Mirror Lakes,
Milford Sound

Whitebait fisherman's Ute at Neil's Beach

Flip flops? Nope. Thongs? Wrong again

Mount Cook YHA

Noah's Ark Backpackers, Greymouth – bikers welcome!

Picton

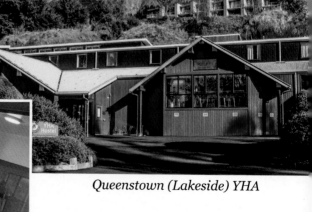

Queenstown (Lakeside) YHA

*Queenstown YHA –
well-equipped kitchen*

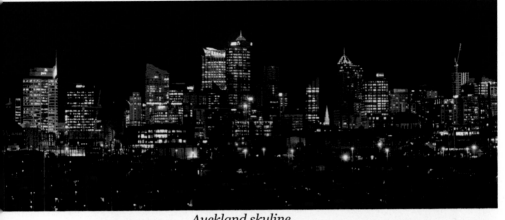

Auckland skyline

On the road from Queenstown

Whangamata

Sheep on the road leaving Mount Cook

Te Nikau Retreat YHA near the Pancake Rocks – so cool!

Bikes at Akaroa Waterfront on a Sunday morning

Pohutukawa MC Tourers at Haast Pass (courtesy of Colin Rowe)

A jolly nice place to stop for a nibble and more on the road to Westport

Bledisloe Campsite near Te Puke

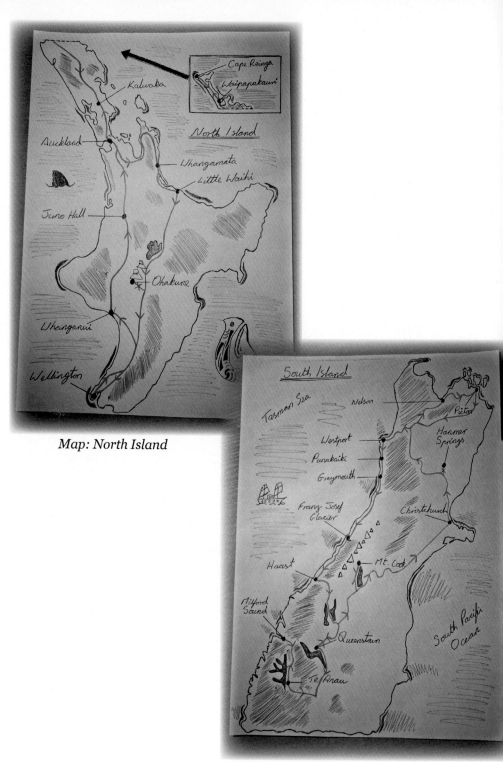

Map: North Island

Map: South Island

Part Two

SOUTH ISLAND: Picton to Te Anau

Day 15: Picton to Westport – 302km

In the morning I took the obligatory photos of The Villa, loaded the car and off I went, bound for Blenheim and the road to Christchurch. How long had I been doing this? Of course that wasn't going to happen. Karma was sticking her nose in again, and the road to Christchurch via SH1 after Blenheim, going south for Kaikoura, was closed due to repair work after the earthquake last year. It must've sustained some serious damage to take this long to fix, but then in a country of less than five million, I would imagine that getting a small army to mend the roads would be a bit difficult, to say the least.

It was decision time. Take the detour and head for Westport, going down the rugged but equally beautiful West Coast, or take the detour all the way round to Christchurch – a *very* long detour around the Kaikoura and Boddington mountain ranges? Westport it was, then.

Coal made Westport what it is. Back in the days when the Brits came out here to dig the black gold, first came the money men and then came the miners, who received the same treatment as they did in the UK. It's happened time and again. I remember from personal experience the miners' strikes of the '80s in my home county of Kent, and the local pit closures at Betteshanger, Snowdown and Tilmanstone.

I made it to St Arnaud and saw a sign at the side of the road with 'Artist' written on it. I thought it was a good excuse to have a change of scenery and a chat to a like-minded soul. Maybe I could pick up a few tips.

Jan Thomson at her Korimako Studio, located in a very modest but spacious house and workshop, was in her kitchen, and, on seeing me, came out to greet me. We shook hands and went into the studio, where I was greeted by her rather appealing watercolours and oil paintings of landscapes around NZ, along with the warmth of her log burner. We sat and chatted about arty stuff and the differences between photography and paintings, and how the web is the way forward for sales – something I really need to start looking into for my own work if I'm going to make a living out of taking photos and the like one day. We swapped cards and said our goodbyes and off I went back to the main highway and onwards to Murchison. What a lovely lady.

The roads were becoming more like tracks now, with frequent single-track sections and overhanging rocks chipped out to incorporate the road. Hawks Crag, a few kilometres from Westport, was an eye-opener; the road goes over a bridge (single lane) and under a cliff, as the river does a U-turn meander, and that's when you think, 'I really need a place to pull over now to take a photo.' In busy times I guess it would be difficult to get back and forth, as you can't see the entire road and just have to take pot luck as you round the corner.

Enter Westport. I did the usual thing of driving around aimlessly until I saw the BP garage, where I filled up and asked for directions to the youth hostel – which, to my surprise, was just around the corner, and it had space, too. The Trip Inn hostel is a very large white house in a colonial style, surrounded by palm trees and other sub-tropical plants, with an equally quaint wood-panelled reception area. The woodworm holes were proof that it was all original – just like the plastering on the ceilings, roses and coving. I was greeted by Donna, who ran the place with her husband, who was an ex-fishing boat skipper. We had a good chat and he explained all the photos of the late 19th-century coal miners covering the walls in the lounge to me, along with how the coal was hewn out of the mountain just outside the town up at Denniston. He was very passionate about the plight of the industry and what the miners went through. His mother was born up that mountain.

One of the paintings I'd seen earlier by Jan, the artist, was of Charleston, which was just down the coast; I remembered her telling me that I should go there, as I am a seafarer and I might find it interesting to see how the ships manoeuvred in and out of the 'bay'. Donna's husband was all too keen to explain how they pulled the ships in by rowing boat and got them through the gap and over the sand bar. If the weather was not just right, the rowing boats would roll over and, well, life jackets were not exactly compulsory back then, and there were plenty of graves dedicated to those who lost their lives chasing the big dollars. How times have changed. The ship would be effectively run aground, discharged and refloated when the tide came back in, then towed back out by the rowing boats. These were hard men for hard times.

After chilling for an hour or so, I had a nibble and then it was time for a pint – sorry, handle. I first went round the corner, as suggested, to the Denniston Dog, which sounded rough but was actually quite a nice bistro-type place. Not for me, though, as I had already eaten. I was after pudding. A bit further up the road I saw the Black and White sports bar and hotel– the bookmakers with beer, just like Bucks in Whangamata. On entering the place, I confirmed what I thought and headed straight for the bar. Everyone was wasted! I had some catching up to do, I thought. Some drunken lads at the bar, locals, started making comments about me when they heard me order, and I thought 'Oh, here we go', but the other members of the group decided to drag their drunken friends away rather than cause a scene. Lucky escape. They had the decency to apologise later, so I forgave them (in my head. I didn't actually *say* it).

While there, I met a single mum of three, who was 24 and *very* recently separated. She was strutting her stuff by the jukebox, but became old news when a busload of Europeans came in from Bazil's Backpackers just as things were winding down. The next thing it was 2am and a fun night was had by all. I know where I'm staying next time I'm in Westport – Bazil's! I popped in and spoke to him on my morning stroll, if only to comment on the fancy artwork all over his property and ask the price. At $32 a bunk it was only a fiver more than the youth hostel. Still, you can't grumble, even at that price.

Day 16: Westport – 40km

And what does one get after a fun night? Yup. A hangover, the way hangovers get worse as we get older, but this one wasn't too bad, and by lunchtime, after a walk around the town and catching up with the words and pictures, I was ready to go out for a little more exploring. During my morning walk, I headed down to the small harbour, where all the fishing boats were moored, and saw a lady in the water under a jetty with a large net. She was whitebait fishing. Donna (it's a popular name down here, apparently) was maybe late fifties, and as soon as she noticed my accent she switched into tourist-information mode, and proceeded to tell me about the whitebait season and how much money a kilo will fetch in Auckland in comparison to down there in Westport. We were just over halfway through the six-week season and she only wanted them for herself and to sell some locally, not on a commercial scale, hence she didn't need a licence. She told me about the white plastic tube she uses to see the fish, as they are see-through, and all the strings and lines she has to raise and lower her kit depending on the tides. She finished off by informing me about awesome photo opportunities of the harbour at night and how to get to the best spot undetected. I bid her farewell and was off back towards my digs.

Back on the food front, I was looking for some meat – but something I could leave in the back of the car all day until I put it into the fridge at my next hostel. I compromised and went for a few chorizos and made awesome pasta and a not-so-awesome casserole/stew-type thing. I often do this when trying too hard at cooking. I put all the flavours in – flavours that don't always go together – and hope that it'll improve the taste, but all it does is make it bland. What the hell – eat it, it's full of vegetables and it's good for you. Effectively, it's medicine. Eat your medicine, fat boy!

Denniston was my evening destination, as Donna's bloke had told me a bit about it and how the view from up there at the coal face was quite something. I decided to go up a bit closer to sunset and kill two birds with one stone.

Twenty-minute drive, my arse! It's 20km each way, and it's up switchbacks. These people must drive like loonies... oh, hang on. They do. And I don't. Not after the episode with PC Plod the other day. My mum wasn't best pleased, I can tell you, when the post arrived with my ticket in it just three days after the offence.

The view was good, but with the cloud cover and a bit of evening mist, the town wasn't too clear, and it made for a pants photo opportunity – so I binned the idea and went for a beer. You can't win 'em all.

Day 17: Westport to Punakaiki YHA – 55km

Early to bed and early to rise, I was gone by the check-out time of 10am, along with all the others, some heading north and some south. I only managed 55km today, as I kept stopping and starting to take photos. Pancake Rocks and the Blowholes are very touristy, so I didn't hang about too long, but I decided to stop at Mitchells Gully Goldmine as it was devoid of tourists and I might learn something useful.

I was a bit short of the entry fee of ten bucks, but the owner let me in anyway as I was indeed the only one there. Dilapidated paths and evidence everywhere that this place hadn't seen any TLC for some time added to the grittiness of it all, and I liked it as I thought it gave a better impression of hardworking land, instead of prettying things up with lights and railings and all that nanny-state stuff. This was a dirty, hard job.

He filled me in about how gold was actually inside the rock, which was like dark sandstone and had to be ground down to release the gold. Unlike actual nuggets, the gold was like powder already, and easily seen in the pan after a brief wash. On leaving to go along the trail for a mooch about, I was warned, 'Don't get gold fever!' It wasn't easy not to look at the earth right there in front of me and think, 'It's gold in there – I can see it!' I could just put a load of rocks in my bag and... What did he say again? Time to move on before I ended up buying an extra suitcase.

Pancake Rocks and the seal colony were just a few places to have a leg-stretch and take some snaps. The seals are 40 metres below on the rocks, and I had trouble with a 200mm lens trying to get them to look more interesting than the driftwood they were lying against. I'd had better encounters with seals, so I decided to move on.

The DOC (Department of Conservation) in New Zealand do an amazing job of looking after all the visitor places up and down the country. You can go into to a public lavatory in the middle of nowhere and find it full of loo rolls and cleaned, and the grass outside has been cut. It almost makes you feel like they did it just for you. There's no doubt about it, this place really caters for tourism.

When I found the little seaside community of Punakaiki, which is more like a cluster of motels and backpackers' hostels on the beach than a proper hamlet, I was overwhelmed by the standard of these places and the care and attention people had gone to in making their place look completely different to the others – oozing the chill-out factor and a relaxing vibe, yet funky and full of character at the same time. And all right on the beach.

The first one I went to had an old 1930's truck in the front garden, painted in the same colour scheme as the house and outbuildings so that you knew it was another 'room' – green and yellow. It really worked. That's why it was full. Punakaiki Beach Hostel is at 4 Webb Street. Check it out. When I told the guy at reception I was a YHA member, he told me to go to Te Nikau Retreat just up the road, a few kilometres over the bridge and back the way I came.

Te Nikau was awesome. Several little outhouses, all of different styles with their own driveways and parking plots. You'd be forgiven for thinking you had just come past a load of private properties, but they were specially built like this. I was in Rata house with another single guy and two couples. Singles slept in the loft, which had space for eight mattresses on the floor. I wasn't too keen on this as, funnily enough, it felt a bit like crawling about in a loft, but there was room to stand. Just.

A few steps down was a lounge commanding the other half of the octagonal building, then down again to two double rooms, then down yet again to the bottom lounge/diner, kitchen and bathrooms. It was so cool. Clean and tidy and all for $24 a night. It rained hard in the night and kept me awake a bit, so I was up early to catch the sunrise, which was a daft idea on this side of the island (the west side), but it was as good an excuse as any to get showered and packed up to go.

I had started writing after breakfast and left with all the others at 10am, but progress was being made and stories didn't write themselves. This writing thing takes some time, you know. I couldn't drive, sleep and take photos all at the same time. Hopefully I'd be able to fine-tune my time management and it would get easier. Of course it would. I have faith in me.

Day 18: Punakaiki to Greymouth – 42km

Today I covered even fewer kilometres than yesterday. I really needed to get my skates on. The car seat wasn't helping my back – which was fine before I left the UK. Too much time on my butt, that's what it was. I tried to walk a few kilometres a day, which helped a lot, but then walking hindered the mileage as it took time out of my day and so the cycle went on.

Greymouth is the biggest town on the West Coast, and the mining capital of the area. I had already heard of Noah's Ark backpackers' hostel, and found it quite easily perched up the hill a bit behind McDonald's (how convenient – I did manage to avoid a visit until the morning I left, but their BLT bagels are just too nice). I tried to find the jade shop before it closed, but was too late as it was a Sunday. There was the old Victorian train station again and all the shops you could need, and if you required any running repairs to your bike, you only had to speak to the owner, Harry, who is an engineer by trade and can weld, change tyres, etc. in his well-equipped garage next door, which can easily hold ten bikes out of sight of prying eyes (few and far between down here, but people like to know their pride and joy is safe).

I overheard him talking to some new guests about motorcycle travel and waited for them to go before I collared him, got myself properly introduced and told him what I was up to.

We struck a chord – almost literally, as he plays bass, too. He told me he was trying to promote the hostel as a place for bikers to stay. They aren't YHA – they're BBH, which is a similar thing but about $8 dearer and not in the AA Guide.

He said I should've come later, as the streets of Greymouth get shut off for the end of October as it's the bike race. What?! I never knew this. It's been running for 27 years and is very popular with riders coming from all over the nation. Sadly, they had their first fatality last year on the first race, but the races continued as planned.

Noah's Ark does have an animal theme to all the rooms, which may take some back to their youth. The artwork on the walls throughout the building is signed and hand-painted to a high standard. The reason it's called the Ark is because it was used as a refuge one year when the town flooded and people wanted to get uphill and away from the rising waters. Originally the building was a Catholic church presbytery, built in 1914, with a church next door that had to be pulled down after an earthquake some years ago – not before the Italian-made stained glass was removed by the church and sent off to who knows where.

It was time to move on and make some distance.

Day 19: Greymouth to Franz Josef Glacier – 198km

After a hearty breakfast, followed by the BLT bagel from McDonald's I'd already promised myself, I headed further south. More twisties and undulating roads, and never a dull moment – but, always careful not to become a statistic, I looked at the distance and driving times and added another fifty per cent, because the going is slow in these sections and the police are never far away with their mobile speed cameras. So watch out! Added to that were regular breaks for naps and coffee, although the naps were increasing as the chance of a coffee lessened, due to the smaller townships and additional scenery – which, by now, was becoming mountainous. It wasn't cold, because I was near sea level most of the time, so sand flies were becoming more of a nuisance. Pale, white-skinned Europeans are their favourite, I think. Sweet blood, they say (as I scratch between sentences).

Just under 200km will get you to Franz Josef Glacier: a town with a glacier. Or a glacier with a town named after it. Either way, both are pretty small, but at least the glacier is free. Hurry up or you'll miss it. The damned thing is disappearing at such a rate that there's a sign along the path after a few hundred metres, letting you know where it extended to not so many years ago. It is quite shocking, and now the tourists and the helicopter rental companies have reached a point where they are chasing the ice and the last few years before it's totally gone and another money-making opportunity dies. This or Fox Glacier just down the road will go first, and then another ghost town will be on the map.

A disappointment was an understatement. I spoke to an Austrian chap who said they have bigger ones where he was from. Never mind. I came, I saw, I photographed and I moved on. Off the main highway and up a road leading I knew not where – but it was a dead end. A dead end with a youth hostel at the end of it. It seemed that karma had decided that my day was done and I totally agreed. Sorted.

Franz Josef Glacier YHA was a lovely place to stay and just a minute's walk from the pubs and restaurants, all charging tourist prices, but good nosh, for sure. The ale was pricey, but fear not, as there is a 4 Square supermarket nearby to stock up with beer, and ample relaxing space around the fire at the youth hostel, where you can cook your dinner and relax on the cheap in the comfy alpine lodge style surroundings.

Day 20: Franz Josef Glacier to Haast Village – 220km

Just before bed I had to get one of the Asian chaps out from his perch by the fire to witness something I couldn't quite understand. I knew the southern lights could be seen from here, but I thought that October wasn't the right time of the year. It was the clouds that were acting funny. Maybe it was just the beer and wine, but he thought it was the moon behind the mountain reflecting off the clouds around the side of it. I agreed, but it did look weird. With a head full of wine and wonder, I went to bed.

Up at 6am and packed and ready to go, I had a chat with a French girl with a Celtic name not too dissimilar to my own who was heading north. Shame we only crossed paths here. We got on like a house on fire.

Never mind. I had wheels to roll and it was time to hit the road and head towards Haast. I wanted to go further but, knowing me, I would find somewhere to entertain myself later on.

I couldn't be more entertained than by a beach with my name on it. After 200km of mountains on one side and beach on the other, ups and downs and all the usual stuff (yes, it's getting a bit tedious now – I'm sure it wouldn't on a bike. It's all about the ride 'n' all that), I finally came to the small township of Haast. There's the beach and the town only a kilometre or so apart, and I went straight to the ultra-modern i-Site to enquire about accommodation. Just around the corner were several motels and two backpackers' hostels, a pub (Monteith's Brewery), a chip shop, a shop and a few houses. It wasn't long before I was in the Wilderness Backpackers, which was all nicely maintained if starting to look a bit tired.

With a really cool lounge area, with greenery, water features and comfy chairs around the outside, along with the necessary kitchen area, there was the option to have single, double or twin rooms, just like a normal hotel but at a premium. I opted for a single with shared bathroom, as it had a desk and I thought it would help me catch up on some writing – at $55. Why not? Just the once is OK. I showered and went out for a nibble and a beer. I settled on the Hard Antler, a Monteith's Brewery pub not too dissimilar from a number of British chain pubs, so I felt at home. The food was cheap enough, too. Cheese and onion toastie and chips went down well for not much more than $10. I saw a helicopter land on the lawn outside, not fifty feet from my table, and saw it was one of the tourist ones. This must be a place where they operate from. I wasn't too bothered about helicopters. I've had my fill of heli rides to get to work, thanks, so it was free when I did it. I shudder to think of what it costs to go up to the glacier in one of them.

Siesta time was followed by an evening drive out to find Neil's Beach, some 40km down the coast towards Jackson's Bay. It was a nice little evening drive, but I did overshoot it and had to double back, as it isn't signposted. I drove onto the beach and was met by a big fellow on a quad bike towing a trailer full of kids over the sand dunes and in between the driftwood. They were having a whale of a time. He stopped and I asked him if I could go on the beach and take photos, as it was my namesake. I had to get a photo of this lot having fun. He just said to keep to the path and, with that, all the kids shouted 'BYE, NEIL!' and waved madly as they sped off on another rollercoaster ride.

I cautiously made my way over the dunes and stones to a place just in front of some whitebait fishermen. After fighting off the sand flies, taking photos of the sunset and the coast and enjoying my time in 'the zone', I made my way back to the car, only to get it stuck in the loose gravel. I knew I should've just reversed out, but the two fishermen were over just as soon as they'd finished enjoying the free entertainment and helped lighten the front end so I could get her out and away from this embarrassing situation. I wanted to ask if I could take their photo, with their fire smoking away and their kit and tent, but thought better of it and buggered off in an embarrassed state. And to think I used to own a Land Rover.

I made it back to Haast in the dark, after pulling over on the way and just listening in to the noises of the night. When they say the jungle/forest comes alive at night, they are so right. In the military, just after dusk and just before dawn are the best times of day to attack your enemy, because the light (or lack of) plays tricks on your eyes – and I know from personal experience that creeping about in the dark, trying not to disturb anything or anyone, is an art in itself. Try telling that to the fat lass who'd just been traipsing around in the room next to me. You'd think she was moving house – the downside of budget travel accommodation. Still, it beats getting cold and wet. "Only stupid people get cold and wet" as my Dad used to say and I haven't proved him wong yet.

Day 21: Haast Village to Queenstown – 216km

After an average night's kip due to the elephant in the room next door, I showered and retrieved my food from the kitchen, all packed into my bag for life from Countdown, New Zealand's answer to Aldi. A cigarette, then into the car and off into the last few hours of the night. I had readied the camera and tripod in case there were any photo opportunities at the side of the road on my way down. There were. Crossing bridges with the snow-covered peaks up above and seeing the roadside waterfalls at Thunder Creek and Fantail, just up the road, was a great start to the day.

Catching the first light of a new day has always brought me as close to any God as I could ever want to be. A new day, new light, new beginnings. There's no excuse not to feel 100% positivity, and anything else that happens in the next 24 hours can be either better or worse than the here and now, so let's make the best of it. Just a bit of my karma, there.

As always, whenever I had an early start, I made good time and covered over 100km in two hours, with the handy speed indicators on every single bend letting you know a safe speed to go round the corner. These are nationwide and, as a new driver (under a year), I found them a great help. Stick to what they say and you can't go far wrong. Just another thing that made driving in NZ such a joy.

Six o'clock turned into eight, then it was nine all too soon and I was in Wanaka at the YHA, booking a bed ahead for Queenstown, where I knew it would be busy and didn't want to be disappointed on arrival.

It was beginning to look like I was becoming dependent on the hostels. I didn't have a problem with that. It's a great way to meet new people, and for what you get for your money it's a complete no-brainer. There are plenty of older people who use them. Maybe ten per cent, but you can always go out or just chill using the free wifi and keep to yourself. One thing's for sure is that you are never short of a tale or two from fellow travellers. I know it wasn't a fully cultural experience, like living side by side with the locals, but I was fulfilling my travel priorities and doing it with some level of comfort. Fair play to those that tent it for the whole time, but I really don't feel that's necessary these days. I'll do it, but only when push comes to shove. It just feels too much like sleeping in a canvas cave to me.

All booked up, and with a coffee in hand, I jumped back into the Beast and headed away from Lake Wanaka, wishing I had stayed a night there instead of in Haast. Hey ho, that's way the cookie crumbles, I guess. I was just too tired to drive the extra 115km from Haast.

I opted to drive over the Criffel Range, via Cardrona, and oh, what a great choice that was. The best bit I remember was the last part as you come out of the mountains, way up high and down all the switchbacks, all the way down towards Arrowtown just before Queenstown. You have to stop here and admire the open valley floor in front of you. You can see for miles, right out to the other end of Lake Wakatipu and the airport. I didn't realise there was an airport there until I saw the Jumbo jet flying below the mountain tops in the valley *below me*, putting the scale of things into perspective. The plane looked like a child's toy in comparison to its surroundings. Epic!

I came to the town centre YHA and asked directions, and I wasn't far out. It was only half a mile around the corner – just close enough to be able to walk into the town centre, but far enough to be away from all the bustle of a town knee-deep in tourists. I checked in a bit early as they had rooms ready, and was in another eight-bed dorm (they get cheaper as the number of berths per room increases – up to about $32, but it also depends on the hostel's location). The bonus of travelling at this time of year was that there was nearly always room, but weekends could be a bit hit and miss.

I enquired about the location of the cheapest pub in town and was told that Bar 1876 (www.1876.co.nz) in the town was one of them. I found it at the end of my nose, after looking around the shops and checking out the array of jade on sale there. I asked a guy from the UK in one of the shops about how the jade was priced, as I was of the opinion that size was all that mattered. It isn't, apparently, but I still wanted a bit of bling to go home with, and settled on a pewter Maori fish hook, which is said to bring safe travel over water. I didn't know this at the time, I just liked it. Safe travel over water? And me a sailor? It was just meant to be. Twelve bucks was more in my price range, too, so I bought it. The jade would have to wait for the 'next time' trip down to NZ.

Bar 1876 exceeded my expectations and, if you've checked out the web address in the back of this guide, you'll see it's not a bad place to sit and watch life go by over a handle or two. And, at $5 a handle, that's not bad going. Maybe it was happy hour,

I wasn't sure. They also did food and, going by what the other patrons were tucking into, I wished I hadn't had the cheese and onion sandwich I made at the side of the mountain road earlier. Still, you can't beat a picnic – even if it is alone.

Queenstown is a gem. A beautiful town in a beautiful setting, mountains all around, along with the lake, make great photo opportunities at any time of year.

There's even a cable car up the side of the cliff, and you're never too far from a bridge where a nice man can help you empty your wallet while you chuck yourself off with your feet attached to the end of a rope. Welcome to the adrenaline-junky capital of New Zealand.

Day 22: Queenstown to Te Anau – 199km

Unfortunately, I wasn't blessed with good luck the next morning, when a big bank of cloud decided to ruin my attempts at getting a decent sunrise photo; I supposed it'd be relegated to the black and white file, where I could make better use of the clouds and moodiness of the whole thing.

Waking up with the rest of a town is always a nice feeling. Watching people on their way to work while the street cleaners are already hard at it. I stopped and asked one of them the way to Queenstown Gardens, where I'd heard I could get some great sunrise shots. He spoke with a Spanish accent and I said 'Gracias' as I went to leave, which only made him stick his head into my window and ask if I was Spanish. He then started gabbling away until I put my hand up and said I only speak a little Spanish –

'poco Espanol, amigo'.

Totally my fault. I asked for that one. I must remember that the only reason everyone else talks English here is because it is such a globally spoken language, and people don't know I'm from England until I tell them. It's pretty obvious when you think about it, but we just assume, us Brits – we can be so lazy.

I was only two blocks away, and when I got there and the sun wa up a bit more it was all cloudy, so I binned the idea. At least I tried. Back to the hostel for a bowl of porridge and a coffee and to get packed for the next leg of my journey. I wondered which way the little car would take me today.

Leaving Queenstown, I had the notion that I should've stayed another day, but time wasn't on my side and I had other places to visit. Gotta keep moving on – story of my life. "Itchy feet", they call it.

State Highway 6 along the east side of Lake Wakatipu is a lovely, meandering stretch with just a few tight turns, and you get an extra few seconds to enjoy the view – but not too much because everyone else is doing the same thing, apart from the locals, who obviously know what it looks like and just want you out of their way so they can get to work.

That's another thing about Kiwi driving. As most of the roads are single lane, if there is traffic right behind you and you're doing the speed limit, do the decent thing and pull in a bit to let them pass. This may seem like I'm teaching you to suck eggs, but it's considered the norm down there. Maybe it's their way of dealing with such narrow roads.

There are a couple of nice little cafés at Athol and Mossburn, which I think are almost identical inside as I stopped at both, one going down and the other on the way back up. Awesome coffee. I have no idea what she put in it, but the Red Bull I had in the passenger footwell wasn't touched, and it kept me going all day. After turning onto SH 94 at Mossburn, it's only a few more kilometres to Te Anau and the beautiful lake of the same name, New Zealand's largest body of water, contrary to what it said in the YHA – the plaque at the lakeside says so. And the man from the council is always right, isn't he?

This turn onto the road to Te Anau to head up to Milford Sound and Fiordland very nearly didn't happen, as my original plan was to get to the southernmost tip of the South Island mainland at Slope Point, and public opinion was that given the choice, Milford Sound wins over Invercargill hands down. So I yanked the Wee Beast around in the road, about three kilometres after the junction, and within a minute I was smiling from ear to ear – I knew I'd done the right thing. The added bonus was that it was about 60km less driving that day.

Te Anau is another quaint, tidy and tourist-driven little township on the edge of the lake, where you can (if the clouds permit) get some great photos of the mountains surrounding it at different times of the day. Sunrise is nice wherever you are, if not just to be by the water on your lonesome listening to the waves lapping and not having to worry about the tide coming in and soaking your feet. I couldn't bear the thought of sacrificing a pair of socks to the water as I only had two pairs with me, and they both had their seat belts on in the back, they were so rigid. If I didn't wash them soon, they'd be walking to the laundrette on their own.

I enjoyed a handle in the Moose Bar just a five-minute walk from the youth hostel on the lakeside, and sat behind the glass wind break (nice touch), watching the sun go down behind the mountains and thinking about dinner, tomorrow and having another handle at $5.50 or something. Happy hour is just after when people finish work. A worker's drink. Still keeping it real. Nice one, New Zealand!

Another night with the same Korean gang I met in Ohakune a week or so ago – I had lost all track of time, rarely knowing what day it was because it didn't matter until a) ferry or b) flight.

Day 23: Te Anau to Milford Sound and back – 250km

Milford Sound is where New Zealand takes on its Scandinavian guise with it's lakes, forests, mountains and very little else and it took a lot of people a long time to dig out the road and the tunnels that will take you there (you'll find all the information on the tourist information boards, which I just photographed to read at a later date because I was in a hurry/lazy). An early start is a must (7am in springtime) to beat the tourists and get the mist on the water of the lakes and the jetties into those lakes with nobody posing with their bloody selfie sticks. If the ducks aren't up yet you can also see glass-flat water, offering perfect reflections of the mountains like at Mirror Lakes. Although small, they do the job if your composition is right. Duck for tea, then.

There are metal grids for draining meltwater across the roads at some points in the mountains, so beware, fellow bikers – these could easily have you off on a bend. I still hadn't seen much in the way of gravel in the middle of the road, although that was probably due to the amount of traffic – which could only lead me to my next thought, that the roads in NZ are becoming more worn due to the number of vehicles on them. Next step could only be widening or heaps of repairs, which were happening right then with the aftermath of the previous winter's (December '16) earthquake, which still left Route 1 between Kaikoura and Picton closed until December '17. Dammit! I'd have to go via the north again.

At Hollyford Valley lookout, or 'Pop's View', I had my first interaction with the world's only remaining mountain parrot. The kea is native to New Zealand, and there are only about

5,000 breeding pairs left. They are on the endangered species list and reputed to be quite intelligent. This was put to the test when I rocked up, alone, nobody else there, just him and me. Well, he acted like a bloke for sure. 'His' mannerisms were so humanlike. I parked and he turned around from gazing down the valley as if to say 'What do you want? Go away, I'm busy.' He bounced along the handrail and jumped down onto the floor, waddling towards me like he was carrying carpets under each 'arm' as if he was a night club bouncer or a body-builder. I was still in the car at this point, taking photos and wondering whether I should get out or not. He looked like a parrot with attitude, and that beak was razor sharp. He heard the door click, looked up at me and stepped back to let me out. What the...? He then turned to look at me, hoping for food, of which there was no chance. I wondered if I could get him to pose from the rock where I was standing, which held a plaque in memory of Robert McAlister Andrew – or 'Pop' – who was killed in an avalanche in 1983 at the age of fifty-two. I put my hand down and patted the rock and he instantly looked over and jumped up on it. Mental!

He then proceeded to pose for a few photos and I was thinking about changing lenses for the 50mm, but thought, 'No. He's not a real model – just use the portrait setting.' He was too camouflaged with the green background, and I lifted my hand in a chopping motion and told him I was going to move around so I could get him against a brighter background. He actually looked behind himself and it was as though he saw the gap in the trees and posed accordingly. This was the most surreal moment of the trip so far. Talk about a humanlike personality. I think I might have even said goodbye to him. He just looked at me and cocked his head as if to say, 'Where's my fee?' Ha. Who's smarter now?

There were more roadworks on entering the Homer Tunnel, and I was surprised when it went downhill quite steeply instead of forwards as I had expected, just like any 'normal' tunnel. That'd be fun for the little car to get back up, with its 30km/h limit and 'no stopping' signs. For me, that translated to 'no stalling'.

There's very little to write about Milford Sound as it is the destination for people planning to go on a boat trip around the Sound – and that didn't include me. That was valuable gas money I'd be using. So after a quick visit to the gents and a beef and chutney sandwich charged at motorway service station price, I left the hordes and started my return to Te Anau. It says to take a few hours getting out there and I took three, given that I was stopping to take photos every few feet, and it took me an hour and three quarters to get back. Sorted. 250km later, I filled up and revisited the Moose Bar, then I chatted with the Koreans at the hostel about their sky dive and how well it went. They said it was awesome. I'm sure it was at several hundred bucks apiece.

I called home to Mum and told her how my day had gone, mentioning that I really needed to get going, as it had taken me eight days to get here from Picton and now I only had four days to get back. I hate having deadlines, but you gotta do what you gotta do, and I had to catch that ferry on time.

Part 3:

Te Anau to Nelson

Day 24: Te Anau to Mount Cook – 419km

Biggest mileage so far today, as I left in high spirits hoping I could make it to either Mount Cook or Twizel by nightfall, and photograph the Southern Alps from the eastern side with the sunset.

I knew I had to go back up to Queenstown. Not a problem, as I quite liked the drive down. I didn't want to go back up the West Coast again as it was so time-consuming, and that was a commodity I didn't have much of. Knowing the way made a difference, as I didn't use the map more than… errm… twice?

I filled up, noted the mileages and was off back towards Mossburn, from where I was served the strongest coffee ever from the café. I don't know how many shots she put in it, but I was buzzing all day and didn't touch the Red Bull in the passenger footwell until the next morning.

It was nice to drive along Lake Wakatipu again, but in the opposite direction, so I could now see what I could only see in my rear view mirror on the way down – and it was just as good in reverse.

When Route 6 goes over the river at Frankton, just before Queenstown, there is always congestion, but they are building a new bridge and the one currently being used is, well, a bit past its sell-by date from what I could see. Always a bonus to see the smiling face of Kiwi road construction from the girls with the 'Stop' and 'Go' signs. They do that all day in the middle of nowhere with the men. All mucking in together. No wonder the women have a 'weathered' look about them. I don't mean that in a derogatory way – just that if they didn't do what they do, the country would only be half finished, wouldn't it?

It was just about 11am, and time to make another wrong turn up a road where I should've known where I was going, but, as is usually the case with me, if I remember my surroundings while on the wrong road I think I am heading the right way because it's familiar. D'oh!

A bit of swearing and a U-turn later, I was in the Burger King car park and ready for a coffee – and maybe a Whopper, which I had to have purely for research, to see if they are the same as back home. I didn't need to stop now until I got to my destination, wherever that may be. Hopefully Mount Cook, or I'd settle for Twizel as second best. We'd see how I felt. The more that happened throughout the day, the more I had to write – and this took longer and I needed to be less tired. It's a hard job this travel writing, you know. Honestly. I was working seven days a week and all I'd done was take photos, write, drive and sleep. Whopper quality consistent, I manoeuvred the Wee Beast out of town.

Leaving Queenstown and up over the other bridge on the Gibbston Highway, if you look to your left you can see the AJ Hackett Bungy bridge. No ta. The Arrowtown hairpin bends were where I was so looking forward to going again, for no other reason than to make the Wee Beast scream in protest at the inclines and turns. No such luck, though, as we were back onto Route 6 and headed for Cromwell along the Kawarau Gorge. It didn't take long at all, and before I knew it I was looking for the exit onto Route 8 to get me up the eastern side of Lake Dunstan, and then I pulled in at Tarras.

It was nothing more than a filling station and a few well-turned-out shops, plus the cleanest public lavvy I had used so far – it was one of those shipping container affairs with all mod cons, and regularly cleaned as it's council owned. Just another little thing that made the journey so much more pleasurable. There was a merino wool shop there, where they sell ready-made garments made from NZ merino wool or you can buy by the ball, so if you're not sure what to take back for that special person who loves to knit – she can make her own jumper. That was Mum's pressie sorted, then.

While in the car park, I could hear organ music being carried on the wind, and looked over my shoulder to see a clump of fir trees about 300 yards away and a load of cars parked in a line. Funeral in the village, then. The lady in the wool shop was amazed when I told her I could hear the music, then we went on to ascertain that I still had good hearing after all those gigs over the years, and that one of us didn't like organ music because he only hears it at funerals, so it reminded him of sad times. Also, that three balls of wool are not enough to make a jumper.

On going back outside, I got chatting to Dave, who was a celebrant. You know – not a priest or a vicar, but someone who is licensed to do all that but without the God thing. He also rode an early '90s Honda CBR1000, one of the first made, and it was looking a bit down in the dumps, too. We spoke about older bikes and if it does the job, why change it – because we want a new bike, no reason, life's just like that – unlike a car, when it's too big, too small, can't afford to run it anymore, and so on. A bike is a toy or a tool – or both in my case. There's always something better, but we do get attached to our wheels, be they two or four.

The Lindis Valley was next, with its big open spaces and sweeping bends, right until you finally come to the foothills and up into the Lindis Pass. This has some great spots where you can pull in, have a brew and marvel at the valley and what you have to drive back down to get to Twizel, via the left hander you'll take at Omarama (I'm not making these names up, they really are genuine).

After a long drive, it can get confusing when looking at road signs, and wrong turns can be made quite easily. I'm sticking with that excuse as it's the best I can muster (other than the truth).

Just another 30km to Twizel, along another open and fairly straight stretch of road, and things were starting to get decidedly alpine now, with the snow-capped mountains in the distance drawing ever closer and the openness of the townships. This might have been a good place to buy some booze and food, as there is absolutely NOTHING up Mount Cook at the township. They call it that – I call it an overgrown base camp, as the only place with booze for the public is at the bar and grill, as the hotels have their own bars and the last shop that was there closed over a decade ago because it didn't make any money.

On the plus side, a 110km round trip up the Route 80 would be so worth it if I stayed at the YHA Mount Cook, at a snip of the price of the competition, and woke up to the magnificent view of the mountain. In thick mist. it was a good job that I took some lovely sunset photos the night before, then. I might have been dog-tired after a 420km day, but boy was it worth it. The highest peak in New Zealand, at 3,754m, right outside my bedroom window. All I needed to do was crane my neck around to the point of injury to see it. Or swap beds with the guy across from me, but he was out of it.

On closer inspection of the lie of the land, it might have been Mount Sefton I was looking at. Oh well. I didn't know any different at the time, so it will still be Mount Cook as far as I'm concerned. I just won't tell anyone, that's all. Denial - it's not a river in Africa.

Day 25: Mount Cook to Christchurch – 329km

After another great sleep and waking up to a room full of other people's farts and smelly socks, I snuck out and made breakfast of my usual porridge with two teaspoons of cinnamon and a chopped-up banana – had to keep the balance right – all washed down with a disgusting cup of that instant coffee I bought in Auckland for ten bucks when I arrived. Then it was time to hit the road and enjoy the sunrise on the mountains.

Seeing the mountains either side of you as you drive back down the valley is awesome – 'epic', even, as they say here. I saw a photographer at the side of the road and looked at what he was trying to photograph – it was only the sunrise, peeking over the mountains in the east. Who'd have thought it? I screeched into a lay-by and congratulated myself for leaving my tripod open for times like these – lazy ones, or just when I needed a speedy, steady hand to grab a shot at a moment's notice. I got it, sort of. It would be better down the valley, I thought, when the sun was over the horizon a bit more and the clouds came into the equation, and I could use my neutral density filter to take the harshness off the sun. Never enough equipment!

As the valley of the Tasman River opened out into the delta that feeds Lake Pukaki, I was granted my request, and was just thinking about stopping when I saw a light on top of a car on some higher ground up ahead. Really? I was only doing eighty. Oh, come on! Oh, hang on – it was orange and it was on a pickup, and there was another pickup on the road coming towards me. He was giving the 'slow down' gesture with his arm out of the... SHEEEEEEP!!! Anchors, first gear and I smiled like an idiot as I crawled past into a road full of freshly shorn sheep. They were laughing at me, I just knew it. 'Bloody tourists,' they muttered, or something very much like that.

After a few minutes of fun and trying to take photos from behind the wheel, I pointed in the general direction of Christchurch and off I went. Left at the bottom of the road and onto Route 8 towards Tekapo and its namesake lake. The terrain started to take on a more Mediterranean feel now, as the greens turned to beige and the trees became sparser. Judging distances and getting the scale of the land became a challenge with no landmarks to work to, reminding me of Dartmoor, but the difference here was that the great bits go on and on, and when they do stop they turn into another great piece of scenery. It's just one great experience after another. We were now in the Canterbury Plains and heading downhill towards the towns of Geraldine and Ashburton, via Route 79.

When I came to the junction in Geraldine, I looked across the road and thought 'Hallelujah! Bikes at last!' and pulled in, all excited, to see more bikes in one place than I had seen on my entire trip. I was greeted with a handshake from a chap on a BMW GSA1200, and instantly started my pitch, unable to contain myself. The poor bugger didn't get a word in edgeways over my first actual chance of making the trip worthwhile. He introduced me to his mates and I told them what I was doing. The Wee Beastie raised a few laughs, as did some of my anecdotes, and cards were swapped. I was told about Akaroa and how bikers like to ride out there on a Sunday along the peninsula road, for an ice cream and a bit of 'Frenchness' at the other end, as Akaroa is the only place the French managed to make a settlement in New Zealand. I should have been able to get some good shots, as the weather was due to be nice. I'd think about it – but I did take some photos of them as they left.

Shortly after they went, I popped inside to take a few photos of the Chequered Flag Bar and Café and have a chat with the owners. I was told about the state of repairs in Christchurch and was given a photo book to look at by the landlord, showing just how bad the earthquake was.

The roads were becoming a bit tedious but, on the good side, the kilometres were totting up quite quickly, as they were long, straight roads with little in the way of junctions, adding to the bonus of feeling a little more positive now after seeing the bikes. If you need to get from south to north quickly, this is the way. Until you get to Christchurch, that is. Just remember to keep your eyes front as you go over the bridges at the deltas of the Rangitata and Rakaia rivers. It's a small reminder of how much water passes under these bridges when it's the rainy season, because right then there was just a stream or two over a few hundred metres of rocks and gravel.

I managed to get to the Rolleston House YHA with only a minor car park kerfuffle, involving me, three car parks and a man in a turban.

The hostel is a listed building, hence there weren't any storage lockers in the rooms, but apart from that it was a good night's kip. The bloke on the bed opposite me had all his stuff in several bags and led me to the conclusion that he was homeless. He looked Maori, but said he was born in Australia. Hmm. I decided not to pry anymore, as he wasn't exactly a chatty type and didn't seem like the happiest bunny in the woods, but he still offered his hand and told me his name. Manners maketh man, they say.

Not much to say about Christchurch itself, as I was quite tired and only managed to get out for a walk around the city centre and see the remains of the cathedral, which, I am told, is to be pulled down soon and replaced, as they couldn't decide what to do with it after the earthquakes. It's just been propped up with scaffolding ever since. It wasn't the only building I saw in the photo book that the manager at the Chequered Flag showed me. The tramlines had sunk as well, and I witnessed that job looking half-done and cordoned off. I'm sure they have their reasons.

The architecture seemed to be a little older than some of the other places I'd seen, or at least it was made to look older, reminding me of home a bit, and I guess that's why I felt less obliged to write about and photograph it. Big cities, are all the same to me, given the odd landmark here and there. They bring out the worst in mankind, for sure.

I went out for something to eat in the first instance and ended up in Mickey Finn's Irish Bar, having shepherd's pie with gravy and an orange juice. Couldn't stand a fizzy beer this time of night, although there was a table of people quaffing Beamish Irish stout. I wonder if it travels any better than Guinness?

I was quite tired again. I needed to have more time to rest and write and explore, as opposed to spending all day on the road and arriving tired, then getting up just as everyone goes to bed and writing until gone 2am. Was I trying too hard? The French girl I spoke to at Franz Josef Glacier told me she only drove for three hours a day. To be fair, so did I, probably, if you took out the naps, the getting lost and the photo stops.

Day 26: Christchurch to Hanmer Springs – 322km

I didn't want to get out of bed – not a good sign, as I was hardly on the pop last night – but I finally left as the market was being set up right outside the hostel. I got a few directions from the receptionist and was off. 'No thanks, mate. I don't need the map. I can remember that.' Who was I trying to kid? I actually managed to get out of town on the first attempt and onto the road the receptionist put me onto to get to the Banks Peninsula and Akaroa.

He only put me on the wrong road! I reset my sat nav for a quick traverse of suburbia to Halswell and onto Route 75. Now all I had to do was follow it until I got to Akaroa. I was told about a few stops along the way, at Tai Tapu and Little River, and stopped outside a farmer's house on a straight bit of road and managed to get a few shots of some boy racers.

I saw a few bikes at the Little River Gallery and Café. Old bikes. Ariels, old Harleys and Enfields, going back to the thirties or even before. One even had a cranking handle. Where did it all go wrong, eh? They were members of the classic car club and didn't have a Facebook page. 'Bugger all that technology' was their answer to my query. Fair enough – I should've guessed, really.

I paid $22 for what turned out to be the poshest cooked breakfast I think I've ever had. There were two slices – as in cake slices – of ciabatta, toasted with olive oil with my creamy scrambled eggs on top, a few handmade potato hash browns, some fresh local mushrooms, a grilled tomato and four Kransky sausages – or little saveloys where I come from – which kind of let it down, I thought, but they did the job in a way, I guess. All washed down with a flat white coffee, which seemed to be the most popular in NZ. No sugar for me, not even sweeteners now. Every little helps.

I didn't take a look in the gallery, but was messaged on Facebook later as I couldn't see the page for the café and I thought it was all one place, so I did a review and said they didn't have mayo, which was my only criticism. Fair play to the girl from the gallery getting back to me with the post, 'We don't serve mayo because we are an art gallery.' D'oh! She saw the funny side of it.

The drive out to Akaroa from there pretty much covered most of the terrain I had already been through in New Zealand, but in smaller chunks. From Christchurch, it's about 75km each way, and it all becomes worth it when you reach the summit of the hill, go around the top and begin your decent, just at the same time as you narrowly miss parking in the Hill Top Café/ Restaurant car park to admire the view. Lush and green rolling hills all around a bay of azure, with a few little islands, yachts – the whole shebang. You can even see Akaroa village on the distant shore. Only a few more kilometres to go. I'll leave it to you to discover Akaroa for yourself. Enjoy, mon ami!

I didn't stay long on the waterfront of Akaroa – just long enough to show a chap a photo I took of him and his missus rounding the corner at the top hoping he would buy it, then have an ice cream, get lost on the way out and shoot off back to where I came, but this time going around the ring road and off up Route 1 until I got to Route 7 at just after Kaiapoi. Then it was all plain sailing for 68km over the Amuri Plain, where the road went back to the flat and brown stuff with some farms thrown in, right up until the foothills started before Hanmer Falls. This was where I turned off onto Route 7a, which is only really there to serve the town of Hanmer Springs. Only another ten kilometres to go.

Kakapo Lodge was the name of the YHA that night. Up the hill on the left and run by a Korean lady and her family, the lodge sat in a great location, with lovely views down the valley. There are also a few other hotels nearby if your budget allows, and even a few RV sites if you're that way inclined. It's kind of a halfway point between Christchurch and the other side of the Lewis Pass, which was, at the time of writing, the only way back to Picton and the north, due to the road still being closed between Kaikoura and Blenheim for repairs after the earthquakes. I had a room to myself again, and no bunk beds tonight as it had proper beds. I couldn't wait to get to bed – or, to be more precise, wake up without banging my head.

A few bikers turned up on old BMW 1150RTs just after me, and I only managed to get talking to them in the morning, just before they left. I mentioned what I was doing and they said they just stayed wherever was cheapest. We were in agreement that YHAs and backpackers were good value for money, and when I mentioned the drying room they looked a bit quizzed. I had to put it to them that in the more remote places, where walkers tend to stay, they have drying rooms. Handy for walkers, but an absolute godsend for a biker to wake up to dry kit if it's the rainy season.

They posed for a few photos and then they were off. Lucky bastards. I'd be back on two wheels next time, make no mistake.

The wasting of kilometres due to backtracking is a bit of a pain, but it's necessary sometimes, and a small sacrifice compared to falling asleep at the wheel and ending up in a ditch.

Day 27: Hanmer Springs to Nelson – 305km

After cooking up two days' worth of pasta the night before, and with the spare garlic bread for the next one, I was gone by sun-up just like the bikers and headed back towards Westport. Or screw it, I'd just head straight for Picton and bypass Westport. I could stop over at Nelson, as was mentioned to me by a guy in a garage, as it breaks up the route nicely – and the route around the coast from Nelson to Picton is, from what he described, very similar to the Coromandel Peninsula: switchbacks, berms, rises and drops. I decided I may as well do it one last time as, when I got back into the north, it'd be motorway most of the way to Auckland.

Over the Lewis Pass and up to Springs Junction, hang a right onto SH85, then right again onto Route 6 and Murchison. A good place to stop for a break, as it's big enough to have toilets, banks and shops, etc., stock up on grub at the 4 Square and off again. There were still a good few clicks to go at this point, so it was a case of sitting back and enjoying the ride until it started getting built up around Belgrove, and then it was 50s and 70s all the way into Nelson City.

A short bout of lostness, via a Golden Arches afternoon 'tea', found me at Nelson YHA on Rutherford Street. I had a fairly standard night's stay and befriended a Finnish girl, who shared the same thoughts on travel as I did. I wondered how she was fixed for onward travel, but on asking she said she was already booked ahead, like everyone else who wasn't keen on hitchhiking. People tend to book up all their travel in advance, with the exception of those few hardcore, who spend their evenings making up a new destination sign to hitchhike to the next day. Most of the hitchhikers I'd spoken to had only waited ten or 15 minutes before getting lucky and being on the road, making new friends with the people fate had put them with for the next few hours. It's generally considered safe to hitchhike in NZ, but I didn't pick any up. When I saw the second hitchhiker I felt bad after driving past her, as I was sure I had seen her the day before at Franz Josef Glacier and felt somehow acquainted with her as we were on the same journey, both travelling the same land, but seeing different things – she had more time to stare out at the scenery for one, as I only had the road to look at (most of the time – you gotta take the odd peek).

Nelson is the 'city of the north' of the South Island and is really nice, or so I am told – you'll have to check it out for yourself when you come down and make up your own mind. There are certainly loads of excursions and things to do there, as many of the folk I met at the hostel stay for at least a few days.

I didn't take the time to write and photograph everywhere I'd been for the simple reason that some places just have to be experienced to be believed. Go there. You won't be disappointed. Everywhere I visited on this trip was on the spur of the moment, and I wasn't disappointed with anything at all – and that says a lot. Actually, one place springs to mind, and another lost the toss between itself and Milford Sound. I'll let you find the answers for yourself.

PART 4:

Nelson to Auckland

Day 28: Nelson to Wellington – 132km

Today I had to catch the ferry at 7pm, with a 6pm check-in at Picton, but first I needed to get there. There is a detour for tourists along the coast, and it isn't unlike the Coromandel Peninsula in its make-up, being coastal, bendy and windy, with ups and downs and switchbacks to keep your feet occupied on the drive.

The distance is actually 108km from Nelson but, as I took the tourist option, it turned out to be longer, but what the hell – as previously mentioned, this could have been the last time I drove like this, as after today it'd be inland, and after that it was all motorway, and after *that* it'll be on two wheels, when I return to do the job as originally intended.

I arrived early, with plenty of time to get some eats from the Thai takeaway recommended to me by a local, which turned out to be delicious and nutritious and well within budget.

After a bit of a debacle with a broken-down lorry on the car deck from the incoming sailing, we boarded nearly 90 minutes late. This forced my decision as to whether to drive onwards into the night from Wellington or stay put and be fresh in the morning.

After a comfortable crossing with other people at the end of their day and just looking for somewhere to doss down for a few hours, I was all awake with a second wind and set about trying to find digs in New Zealand's capital – no, it isn't Auckland, like many think.

Straight off the ferry in Wellington, you turn left out of the quayside, and directly across the road (opposite the train station) is Hotel Waterloo and Backpackers. According to Google, it was about $25 a night, which seemed about right, but it may as well have been $100, as that night it was full and there was no room at the inn for this weary traveller.

I settled for the Lodge in the City, which was considerably expensive for a two-star property, but what character! I was too late for drinks from the garage, as they didn't sell alcohol at all. It seemed I was misinformed, so I had to go into town instead for a few scoops. Bummer. I went two blocks down Taranaki Street to Courtenay Place, where I found a good number of drinking parlours open till 4am. FOUR AM! On a Tuesday?! These people really don't care about their jobs.

I was well looked after by the locals, had a few beers and chatted away with people from all over on working holiday visas. It's interesting to see things from a local perspective for a change, as you get to know a place a bit better – especially if you intend to move there. Maybe. The 'maybe' was turning more into a 'probably not', sadly, after my chat with the people at the Seamen's Union.

A Facebook update along the lines of 'I'll be in bed by 4am' evolved into a real-life sentence of 'I'll have a rum and coke, please, mate', but I was quite surprised that I actually did get back around four, probably due to the efficiency of the bouncers. It was almost as though a 'drinking up time' wasn't heard of there. It's literally 'Drinks inside, please', and everyone moved pretty bloody quickly. I joined them, and within ten minutes we had all left the bar. The serving of drunken types is not tolerated at all in New Zealand, so if one of your party is a little worse for wear you may as well save yourselves the embarrassment and head home. It seemed that using prop forwards as doormen had the desired effect. They're big fellas those Fijians and Samoans. Respect.

By all accounts I had a really good kip, and woke for a cold shower to shake off the last of the rum before breakfast. While in my room, I happened to take notice of the radiator. A rarity in this part of the world, as I am told it was mainly the Brits who installed them. If you're cold in your room in NZ, use a blanket – there are always plenty available in every accommodation. Keeping it old school, it's cheaper, but don't even think of using your sleeping bag. The spread of bed bugs is closely monitored here, and use of your own bedding is not encouraged anywhere.

I digress. Back to the radiator. Probably the best photo of the trip: a radiator with a chair. I had to sit on the floor and lean right back to get the angle right, and an awesome black and white was born. I knew it was a good idea to stay there.

I took a few more photos of the place and mentioned it to the Asian owners, who gave me the green light to post to Trip Advisor shortly before I packed the car and left heading north. In the wrong direction, the same way I went on arrival the previous night, cursing as I went. At least I knew where to do my U-turn.

Day 29: Wellington to Whanganui – 223km

If I timed it right, I still had another three days' worth of driving in the North Island before the car was due back in Auckland on the afternoon of the 20th, so I could afford a bit of a detour and visit one or two of the places I had previously earmarked to take photos and bed down for the night. I chose Whanganui as I had heard about it having lovely sunsets and being a 'city' by Kiwi terms (more people than sheep per square kilometre?), and it was about the right distance away from Wellington. All boxes ticked, I was headed for Whanganui, then.

Back over old ground once more. I could've gone up SH56 to Palmerston North and across on SH3, but it didn't inspire me and just made for a longer day. I quite enjoyed crossing the river estuary at Foxton again, anyhow.

I was in familiar territory, so I just sat back, put on some comfy tunes and wound my way north, counting back down the page numbers on the map. Every turn of the page was a little 'Yay' in my head, as if I had achieved another milestone. Another page closer to Auckland and the journey home. The return journey could hold some as yet unseen surprises – and I wasn't wrong.

I loved the way everything still had that pioneering, frontier town look about it. The shop signs with the livery on the front – but when you look closer from behind, they're just a load of plywood with batten on the back, which reminded me of the set on Mel Brooks' *Blazing Saddles*. It was no stretch of the imagination to take things back to the 1860s when the town was founded, but with the horses now gone in favour of the pick-up trucks they refer to as "utes" in NZ and Australia.

The Tamara Lodge BBH was my choice for that night – another lovely, large colonial family home overlooking the Whanganui River, as the youth hostel wasn't taking check-in until 4pm. Their loss, you can't win them all.

I went into town for a mooch about and came across a bird with yellow rings around its eyes and a strikingly beautiful plumage. About the same size as a blackbird, but with a longer tail and a dark green head and yellow legs, I had to ask the ladies locking up the i-SITE what it was. 'Australian import – it's a myna bird,' she informed me. One snap was all I got before he was off. Another box ticked, a little grin of achievement, and it was time to get back to the digs for check-in.

A young British girl from Brighton – the resident Woofy – was running the place, as the owners were away.

I checked in at the same time that another two British girls turned up and were asking for directions into the main street – the imaginatively named Victoria Avenue – and places to eat, etc. We were also told about the great photo opportunity up at the war memorial across the river at Durie Hill. There was an elevator, too. I drove. Camera in hand, I went up the watchtower for a great panoramic sunset of the town, with the sun running off into the Tasman Sea. Job done.

I descended into the town and had a walk around, admiring the old cinema, which is still a cinema and not a theme/chain pub or bank – which was nice. I was surprised to find a little the town in 2005, while across the road sat a few homeless fellows with their night's central heating encased in brown paper bags. Such a shame. Not for me to comment, I suppose. I was a guest there and, as much as I would have liked to, I couldn't change anything. It was just the constant reminder of how things are there. It's not like the streets are overrun with homeless people, but it is there, just like everywhere else in the world – but nowhere near as bad.

I shared a dorm with a French bloke, who was hitchhiking around the country to save money. My third brush with the bravest of the backpack elite. Fair play to him. I was going the other way – otherwise he would've needed to change his sign. Some company would have been nice, as he was an interesting guy. Oh well, looked like I'd have to put up with more of my singing, and that is something that no living being should have to endure.

Day 30: Whanganui to Juno Hall, Waitomo – 277km

Just lying in bed, waking up to the sounds of the tuis in the garden, with their absolutely captivating birdsong, and planning how I would go about readying myself for that day's drive wound me up ready for action and then – boom, I was out of bed like a shot, before I remembered the poor French bloke in the bunk opposite. Damn! Had to slow down and make less noise or he'd...

'Oh, bonjour! I thought you were asleep. I'm off soon, so have a good one, man.'

He just grunted something like 'OK, man, see you later. Have a safe trip', rolled over and went back to whatever cheese he was dreaming about.

Sweet – green light. Packed and out of the room in five minutes, I piled my stuff into the bathroom, which was just next door and empty at this hour. I showered and made for the kitchen to rustle up some porridge and a cup of that disgusting coffee. For $9 for 100 grams, you would like to think there would be *something* resembling a drinkable quality, but no. The day that starts with a bad cup of coffee is not a good day, so after I had wiped the condensation from the windows of the Wee Beastie, I made for the nearest garage where I could find the antidote in the shape of a decent cuppa.

That was me sorted. Gas, coffee and porridge – let's rock! I was in high spirits that morning for the simple reason that, as the day was bright and clear, I might get a good view of Mount Tongariro on the way up the west side of the country. But first I had to negotiate my way inland via SH4 and follow the road through forests, farms and open country, as it winds its way over the 24km towards the Aberfeldy School. Soon after this, I was following the Mangawhero River for a trip down memory lane to old geography lessons about rivers and words I hadn't used in years, like 'meandering' and 'oxbow lake' and then finally 'tributary', as it is joined near Raetihi by the Makotuku River, with its source way up in the mountains. I enjoyed following the meandering snake, as it feeds the valley floor with life and keeps the grass green and the livestock happy, criss-crossing its many bridges, but now it was time to move on up into the hills – fingers crossed and my camera in its usual place ready for any photo opportunities.

I could've turned right there onto SH49 and headed straight for Ohakune and the Station Lodge YHA again, but with so many places as yet unvisited, going back over old ground seemed a bit daft, so I went up into the hills and past the few little villages on my way towards National Park. At the same time as being a park name, it is also a township spread back on the west side of the road, and on the right for the last few miles I had been getting the most awesome views of Mount Tongariro and Mount Ngauruhoe, which had been obscured by bad weather and cloud cover on my last visit all those weeks ago.

The views were getting better as I drove onwards, and when I came to a stop at National Park gas station, I could see the two mountains with their white peaks nicely separated by SH47. It might have made a nice panoramic, so I made the effort to take the necessary photographs and enjoy the moment before moving on towards my next stop. Where that was likely to be, I didn't have a clue – I'd just look at the map and then decide.

My initial plan – and I use the word in the loosest of terms – was to make it to Hamilton and stay there, but I wanted one more night in the countryside and plumped for Waitomo and the YHA/BBH at Juno Hall instead. That'd do nicely.

There were glowworm caves nearby and I thought I might visit them. I had been told several times on my trip about people having glowworms in their gardens. This kinda put me off the idea of giving someone $50 to go into a cave and then not be allowed to photograph them because cameras kill them – really? However, the Waitomo Glowworm Caves experience did include a boat ride through the caves, and if I had looked at their website before coming I might have paid a visit. On second thoughts, if I did that with everything I had been told about, I would've run out of cash before I even got to Wellington. Fifty bucks was two days' digs or two-thirds of a tank of gas, so I just added it to the list of things to do next time I was back in NZ.

Staying on SH4 right up until its empty junction with SH3, as it comes in from the west and New Plymouth, I turned right onto SH3 and up towards Te Kuiti, which was halfway along the last 30km of the day. I stocked up in the city with food and a few bottles of ale for the evening, and finished my drive with a slight detour off SH3 onto SH37 for the last few kilometres to the hostel.

With its driveway well-positioned on a left-hand bend and at a good incline, I went straight forwards, ignoring the bend, and up into the parking area, almost as though it was an emergency escape lane. 'That'll be fun getting out of in the morning,' I thought.

I parked the little Mazda next to a beat-up old Subaru station wagon in the car park and was greeted by a little dog and the words, 'Hello, young man. Are you here to check in?' I looked around and couldn't see anyone, so I replied to the pooch, 'Oh, you must be Brian, the talking dog receptionist.'

So we had a comedian on site. Great. That should make the evening more memorable. Then a face appeared from the back door of the laundry and I was greeted by a strong-looking farm-hand-cum-hostel-warden in his mid-fifties with his hand held out towards me. 'Alright, man?' I said, as we shook and exchanged pleasantries, before I was ushered inside into the alpine lodge and its comfy open-plan reception area and lounge, the kitchen separated just by a small supporting wall along one side and a large log fire, feeding an equally large chimney pipe up to the ceiling.

He mentioned the navy and I could tell straight away that he didn't mean the merchant. 'The real Navy,' he said – they always say that. 'I used to blow things up for a living' – little did he know, so did I, but this wasn't a game of toppers. I wasn't there to argue whose dad was biggest.

I was all checked in and in my room in a few minutes, and was told that if I was about at 5.30pm, I could help feed the lambs their milk. Cool. I'd never bottle-fed a lamb before. I was then given a tour of the grounds and introduced to the deer they had purely because she was orphaned after her mother died while giving birth to her a good few years ago, and it seemed the decent thing to do. There was also Dot the blind ewe, going 'BAAAAH!' on the skyline in answer to her lambs' calls for food, plus the three little pigs. Only they were not so little, with littl'un up the top of one hill, with his dad and mum down the bottom, in with the lambs. The story went that even though littl'un was only eight months old, he was still sexually active, and had to be kept separate from his mum. 'Well, look at the knackers on him at his age!' said my host.

Pops had a bit of a temper and that was the other reason for his isolation. Those tusks were about four inches long, and I was told not to put my hand anywhere near his head or he'd have the long, pointy things with nails on, which I value so much, for a snack. They were kept in by an electric and wooden fence so they couldn't get close enough to dig down and burrow out. Another method of avoiding the ground being turned into a quagmire was the nose rings they had. There were also feral pigs in the area, who came onto the land and foraged at night, and who usually met their maker when there were shotguns waiting in the bushes for when they came round for a visit – BANG! Sizzle, sizzle... Goodnight Vienna, hello bacon sandwich. Country folk with country ways.

The view from the top field and the tennis court was of lush, green, rolling hills in a small valley, but fitting for my last night in the New Zealand countryside, and I didn't regret one iota coming here.

Just out the back of the lodge was a small pool, which wasn't in use when I was there, but I was sure would be in the summer months, with gardens all around where you can pitch a tent if you're that way inclined, as did a young couple in love whom I met when it was lamb feeding time. Everyone mucked in and it was a pleasant experience for all. Another box ticked, but not one I had envisaged ever experiencing. "It's all part of life's rich tapestry" is what my Mum says. Too true.

Soon after the feeding, some middle-aged German ladies arrived and were informed at reception about the free transport available at 6pm to take them, should they wish, to the village, where they had a very reasonably priced menu and drinks at the pub. Top-class tourist hospitality right there without breaking the bank. Me, I cooked my own, had a bottle of wine and got down to typing up another few pages and looking at the day's photos. I was now in the habit of doing this as a routine (I had to treat this a *bit* like a job if I was ever going to get it finished).

There were four of us in my dorm when it was time to turn in, and I was amazed that the German guy opposite me had to be separated from his girlfriend – they're not all mixed rooms, reminding me of the line in the Who song "Naked Eye". Come to think of it, I've never seen any mixed dorms while in the UK. Typical. The old British stiff upper lip and all that.

So that was it, I guessed. Up with the lark in the morning and the last leg north to Auckland, bypassing Hamilton, but right now it was sleep time, with a smile on my face and time to reflect on my awesome trip in this beautiful land.

Day 31: Waitomo to Auckland – 194km

After a hearty breakfast of things I ended up buying again in Auckland later that day, due to a certain someone leaving his Countdown 'bag for life' full of food at the hostel, I hit the road in the wrong direction and started towards a dead end, then turned around and began a tedious day of motorway driving in a northerly direction, back to where it all started – Auckland.

Skirting Hamilton and coming on and off SH1 a few times to beat the traffic, I followed the trucks and other traffic back into the city, where I had originally planned to stay at the other YHA just a block or two away from the City Hostel – the International Hostel. Full. Both of them. Back to my tablet for a recap on what else was available, and I found the Silver Fern Backpackers, conveniently just off the motorway at the top of the city.

Not quite as refined as the YHA but much more friendly, with the usual mix of nationalities, although the clan from Luton, UK, made it that little bit more fun, as they were in full party mode as I arrived, drinking, smoking and generally mucking about. This was going to be a great place to spend my last few days in NZ. Chill out, have a beer or three and get the writing finished. Or as near as finished until the ale took effect and I joined the party, at least.

Nikki, on reception, with her locks of pure ginger and in her combats and short t-shirt, was on a year's trip. She worked at the hostel until her colleague took over, then she went into party mode with her pal, Roz, also from Luton. Then there was Chris, a marketing graduate from Shropshire and a big rugby fan, lounging around in his tight shorts – a bit too tight for a chunky chap, but it was warm and he was a good laugh.

Then I heard them mention this bloke called Barry, whom I hadn't met. A bespectacled 20-something American and quite an oddball fellow, but a massive laugh factor and *definitely* someone you need to have around if the party isn't going with a bang. He built a cocktail bar out of three pieces of wood screwed together in the most haphazard manner I had ever seen, and was making cocktails for us all of just rum and ice and mint and... errm... yup, that was about it. The owner wasn't pleased when he came in, and Barry was told to take it down, but as he wasn't charging for the drinks there was little he could do to stop our Barry from being the centre of attention.

I had found some Kiwi Tripel in the off-licence at the top of the road, and at nine per cent it looked good on the bottle. It reminded me of my Special Brew days and, as I wasn't quite drunk enough to enjoy it, it stayed behind the sofa until it was required later. Fortunately, it wasn't. A pale imitation of what is otherwise a nice sipping beer from Belgium – and that's where I intend to get it from next time.

We had the evening to kill and decided that, as it was my last night, we would 'nip out to Father Ted's for a few'. How uncanny. Back to the beginning.

This was my story but you'll have yours, and I can pretty much guarantee that, however you choose to go about this beautiful country of just about every different type of terrain from beach to mountain, you'll have a ball, whether it's on mountainous, sheer-drop hairpin bends on ice, throwing snowballs before going to the beach, surfing, throwing yourself from perfectly good masonry, walking in the sub-tropical rainforests or just chilling out.

How much did it all cost?

Now the boring bit – or, for some people, the best bit, as planning and preparation are key to the perfect holiday, aren't they? At the time I went, one NZ dollar would get me 56 British pennies.

Overall budget: £4,000

Door to door. If my memory serves me right, it kinda broke down like this:

Flights: £800

That was return from London Heathrow to Auckland with Cathay Pacific. Next time I'll go the extra mile to Christchurch and do it the other way around to mix things up a bit. Cathay Pacific were awesome and I couldn't get enough nibbles and drinks in, although I rarely drink alcohol on a flight, just the odd beer. I was down for one meal each way and ended up with double that and more. Thoroughly recommended. I booked about a week in advance and went from mid-September to the back end of October, just as winter turns into spring in NZ and before all the hordes come. This was probably the reason for a lack of bikes on the road, too.

Car hire + bond: £650

No credit card needed at Usave, just use your debit card or even cash. Most other rental companies won't do this. The little 1.2l Mazda Demio may be New Zealand's most stolen car, but don't let that stop you. An awesome little car for what it is, just don't spend too much time on the steep slopes, as that 1.2l engine is a bit on the gutless side – and I was one-up, remember. If there are more than two in your party you would need something bigger, and there's heaps of stuff out there second-hand. I saw plenty of other camper hire companies, so don't think it's all just 'Jucy' campers.

Fuel: £350

Or thereabouts, given that I almost emptied the tank and it took $82 to brim it to the top at an expensive garage. I usually filled up for somewhere between $68 and $75, as I didn't go into the reserve again after that experiment to work out my MPG. The Little Beast returned 600km from a full tank. Total distance travelled by car was 5,997km over 25 days.

Accommodation: about £370

Based on about $25–32 per night over thirty-one nights. Mostly, I stayed in YHA or BBA accommodation, but I did camp on two occasions for a bit less – pound for pound, you get better value at a hostel, but then some won't like the sharing-room thing, with other people's farts and feet. Camper hire would dramatically reduce this, but then I like meeting people. It all comes down to how much time you have. Ideally (apart from biking it), I'd rent a camper and stay somewhere I could shower, etc. every three days or so (minger).

The other £1,830 went on food and beer, of course, but that figure now seems a bit high. I don't know - I wasn't counting. I vaped, as there are lots of outlets for vapers in NZ – mainly the bigger cities, but I do remember seeing the juice on sale at service stations and, as mentioned right back at the beginning, cigarettes are *very* expensive in NZ.

I hope I have inspired some of you to go to this spectacular country, which has so much in common yet, at the same time, is so different from my homeland in the UK – and it's about as far away as you can get. If just one of you go to New Zealand after reading this, then my job is done.

Useful Links

In order of the places I visited here is a list of useful links:

1: **Scootling Scooter Hire, Auckland**

www.scootling.co.nz

2: **Pohutukawa Motorcycle Tours**

www.pohutukawatours.com

3: **Lonely Planet Guide Books: New zealand**

www.lonelyplanet.com/new-zealand

4: **Thomas Cook Travel**

www.thomascook.com

5: **Cathay Pacific Airlines**

www.cathaypacific.com

6: **Asda Travel Money**

https://money.asda.com/travel-money/

7: **Father Ted's Irish Bar, Auckland**

www.fatherteds.co.nz

8: **Usave Car and Truck Rental, Auckland**

www.hirecar.co.nz/

9: **Kiwi Maps Pathfinder - New Zealand**

www.kiwimaps.com

10: **BBH Backpacker Hostel Network, New Zealand**

www.bbh.co.nz

11: Youth Hostels Association of New Zealand

www.yha.co.nz

12: Baldrock Farm Stay, kaiwaka

www.facebook.com/BaldrockViewFarm/

13: Bucks Sports Bar and Grill, Whangamata

www.bucksbar.co.nz

14: Bledisloe Camping

www.bledisloeholiday.co.nz

15: New Zealand Roads information

https://nzta.govt.nz/traffic-and-travel-information/

16: Waiouru Army Museum

www.armymuseum.co.nz

17: Ohakune Éclair Shop

https://www.facebook.com/johnnynationschocolateeclairshop

18: i-Site Visitor Information

https://www.newzealand.com/int/visitor-information-centre

19: Bluebridge Ferries

www.bluebridge.co.nz

20: Korimako Art Studio

www.korimakostudio.com

21: The Denniston Dog Bar and Restaurant

www.dennistondog.co.nz

22: The Black and White Sports Bar and Hotel, Westport

https://www.facebook.com/The-Black-and-White-Hotel-62381418990/

23: Mitchell's Gully Gold Mine

http://mitchellsgullygoldmine.co.nz/

24: Monteith's Brewery

www.monteiths.co.nz

25: The Hard Antler, Haast

https://www.facebook.com/HardAntlerBarHaast/

26: Bar 1876, Queenstown

www.1876.co.nz

27: Moose Bar, Te Anau

http://www.themoosebarteanau.com

28: AJ Hackett Bungy

https://www.bungy.co.nz/

Just a little twist at the end of my tale

As karma would have it, I finished writing this guide while sailing on a tug boat from Cork, Ireland, bound for delivery in Istanbul, Turkey. This took me past Italy and Greece... so it looks like I got to have my cake and eat it.

Go safely, now! Until next time - CHEERS!

Neil

Disclaimer:

While every attempt has been made to ensure that all of the information in this guide book is correct, I am only human and mistakes happen. Prices change and so on, so please feel free to use other sources of information for confirmation, as I would hate to be held responsible for any misery or loss caused to you during your time in NZ. All opinions are the opinion of the author and not necessarily a statement of fact. And remember: Getting lost is where the adventure begins.